BEFORE JESUS COMES...

He is the root and the descendant of David, the bright morning star

ALI METTAU-RAS

JILCO MINISTRIES
CLINTON, BC
CANADA
2018

PREFACE

In the Spring of 1968, as I was seeking the Lord, He answered and began to teach me in a very special way. The first lesson He gave me concerned His Name. Up to that time I never thought much about the Name of God, but now that Name started to live and become very important.

I asked the Lord to teach me what was important to Him for us to know in this day and age. First of all He drew my attention to *His Name*!

Secondly, He directed my attention to *Jerusalem*, the place where He wants to return to. He explained to me that He once again desired to accept Israel as His holy people and to restore the priesthood to them. I had never thought of Israel as priests. However, this seemed to be of importance to God's future plans.

Next the Lord directed my attention to the *two peoples*. His desire is to join the Gentile Christian church and Israel into one.

But before He does this, He wants to use the Gentile Christian church to provoke Israel to jealousy. Now I had heard about this before. In my youth I had been taught that we were supposed to make Israel jealous. But the Lord put a different spin on this. He explained to me that He Himself is going to make Israel jealous and in this process will use us as well. So, it will be His sovereign act, He is the one that will do it.

During His teaching, the word *witness* lit up. Israel is God's witness. The Church too is His witness. The Lord has prepared Himself two witnesses, witnesses of His great and mighty deeds.

The authors of the Bible do tell us about God's mighty deeds. They had an eye for what He was doing. I asked the Lord: "Where can I see you in action in our present time?" The Lord answered me: "Watch what My Spirit is doing in the Church and in Israel."

To my surprise He also showed me that today Israel had not received the promised land with His blessing, but that Israel herself had tried to bring about the fulfilment of His promises. That is why there is no peace in the Middle East.

The Lord desires unity among the believers, but He does reject the unity the World Council of Churches is contending for.

I started to ask the Lord for prophets. After all, the Lord has not changed! If He called forth prophets in the past, why not today? The nations and the Church are so confused, the Lord has to call forth prophets. So, I prayed for a prophet for the Church and one for Israel.

The Lord assured me that He would give *prophecy*.

Half a year later, in the fall of 1968, the Lord, again in answer to my prayers, brought me into contact with the prophetic message of Rev. Leenhouts. In his books I found back all these subjects, but clearer and more extensively. I learned much from him.

When I present here a Bible study about the coming days then no doubt much influence can be found from his prophetic message. Specifically, this is the case when I touch on the book of Revelation. However, I must put this down in my own words and the way I understand it.

In hindsight, I notice that at that time the Lord did not draw my attention to His return. Apparently, the return of the Lord is not one of the first things we should look for in our days. Specifically, my attention was directed to everything that as yet has to be fulfilled *before* the Lord returns. Yes, Jesus will come back, that is certain. He said: "Behold, I am coming soon." But this 'soon' has already lasted for more than two thousand years. This should warn us that the Lord experiences time differently than we do. Measured in eternity, these two thousand years are but a few days.

When in our time the call goes forth that Jesus is about to return, we should not be tempted to lose sight of what must yet happen before He does come back.

With the expectation of the return of Jesus we should keep in mind several aspects to have a biblical view of the future.

We should not think too little of the HOLINESS of Jesus, nor should we make light of the LOVE of Jesus.

Furthermore, we also should not make light of the WORTHINESS of Jesus' death on the cross, nor expect too little of the POWER of His shed blood.

We must not separate Jesus from the Name YHWH!

We should without bias PUT TO THE TEST visions of the future against all biblical testimony.

A. Mettau-Ras, 1995

THE HOLINESS OF JESUS

GOD IS HOLY

Israel knew and experienced God as holy and to be feared, an awe-inspiring and dreadful God. The best way Israel could picture God was to compare Him to fire. He is as fire. "For the Lord, your God, is a consuming fire, and a jealous God." Dt. 4:24; Heb. 12:29.

This is how Israel experienced God. "Now the appearance of the glory of the LORD was like a devouring fire on the top of the mountain in the sight of the people of Israel." Ex. 24:17. God manifested Himself in the fire and spoke from out of the fire. "Did any people ever hear the voice of a God speaking out of the midst of the fire, as you have heard, and still live?" "Out of heaven he let you hear his voice, that he might discipline you. And on earth he let you see his great fire, and you heard his words out of the midst of the fire." Dt. 4:33, 36. See also: Dt. 4:11, 12; Ex. 19:17-20 and Dt. 5:4, 22.

Israel feared God, stood in awe of Him and was afraid of His fire; Dt. 5:25; Dt. 18:15; Ex. 19:18, 19; Ex. 20:20.

Israel's God is a holy God, the one and only God, incomparable and far above all other gods. He is a God who acts to save His people from the power of His enemies. This is what Moses sang when Israel came out of Egypt, "Who is like you, O LORD, among the gods? Who is like you, majestic in holiness, awesome in glorious deeds, doing wonders?" And in Isa. 40:25 the Lord says: "To whom then will you compare me, that I should be like him?"

No one can see God and live (Ex. 33:20). That is why God hid Himself in the cloud for Israel's protection, so they would not die because of His holiness. Ex. 19:9, 16; Ex. 34:5. Sinful man over against this holy God is like gasoline over against fire.

HIM YOU SHALL REGARD AS HOLY!

The true believers in Israel remained impressed with God's holiness and awesomeness. For example, we see Moses admonishing Israel: "For the LORD your God is God of gods and Lord of lords, the great, the mighty, and the awesome God, ..." Dt. 10:17, and Joshua warns the people: "You are not able to serve the LORD, for he is a holy God. He is a jealous God ..." Jos. 24:19.

In Psalm 99:9 David exhorted the people to "exalt the LORD our God, and worship at his holy mountain; for the LORD our God is holy." Asaph too trembled before God when he pondered His deeds: "But you, you are to be feared! Who can stand before you when once your anger is roused?" Isaiah is startled when he sees the Lord in a vision: "Woe is me! For I am lost; for I am a man of unclean lips, and I dwell in the midst of a people of unclean lips; for my eyes have seen the King, the LORD of hosts!" Emphatically he directs Israel to pay attention to God's holiness: "But the LORD of hosts, him you shall honor as holy. Let him be your fear, and let him be your dread." Isa. 8:13.

JESUS IS HOLY

We believe that in Messiah Jesus God was manifested in the flesh. In order to walk among us and dwell with us He laid down His divine glory so that His holiness would not harm us and in love for us He emptied Himself and took on the form of a human being. Phil. 2:6, 7.

Yet, notwithstanding that He humbled Himself and emptied Himself of His divine glory, He remained holy. Not in the sense of awe-inspiring and terrifying, but in the sense of irreproachable. Actually, the meaning of holiness is to be set apart, separated for a specific purpose, being totally different from all others, unique.

Jesus was set aside in order to receive God's burning wrath, so that whosoever would believe in Him would escape the wrath of God, because Jesus already has born God's punishment for him.

From the moment Jesus was taken up into heaven He once again was clothed with this awe-inspiring, fearful and fiery holiness which He had with the Father before He came to earth. When Jesus ascended he was hidden from view by a cloud for the protection of the disciples, as a cloud did for Israel on Mt. Sinai.

"God has highly exalted him and bestowed on him the name that is above every name." Phil. 2:9. And according to Eph. 1:20, 21 we may know the immeasurable greatness of God's power, "that he worked in Christ when he raised him from the dead and seated him at his right hand in the heavenly places, far *above* all rule and authority and power and dominion, and above every name that is named, not only in this age but also in the one to come." As High Priest He now is "holy, innocent, unstained, separated from sinners, and exalted above the heavens." Hebr. 7:26.

In Rev. 15:3-4 He is worshipped as the holy King: "O King of the nations! Who will not fear, O Lord, and glorify your name? For you alone are holy."

JESUS' FIERY COMING ON THE LAST DAY

How much more awe-inspiring and unbearable must be the appearing of Jesus when He comes, not just in a vision, but in reality! Peter says that at the coming of the Lord the earth will be burned up. When people scoff at the long-time coming of the Lord he writes in 2 Pet. 3:7 and 10 "But the heavens and earth that now exist are stored up for fire, being kept until the day of judgment and destruction of the ungodly. (…) But the day of the Lord will come like a thief, and then the heavens will pass away with a roar, and the heavenly bodies will be burned up and dissolved, and the earth and the works that are done on it will be exposed."

The return of the Lord will make an end to our earthly, human time and history. Jesus will come on the very last day of our chronology.

Furthermore, Peter mentions in 2 Pet. 3:15, 16 that Paul too wrote several times concerning these things. Although it might be hard to understand what he wrote, and some have twisted it to their own destruction, yet it always dealt with the same things as what Peter wrote about, namely the things of the last day when Jesus comes.

When Paul wrote in 2 Thess. 1:7-8 "…to grant relief to you who are afflicted as well as to us, when the Lord Jesus is revealed from heaven with his mighty angels in flaming fire, inflicting vengeance on those who do not know God and on those who do not obey the gospel of our Lord Jesus," it is about the same day of His return, the last day of earthy time and history.

And when the author of the letter to the Hebrews writes that the Lord once more will shake the heavens and the earth… "for our God is a consuming fire," then too it concerns the last day.

Jesus describes His coming as lightning that shines from the east as far as the west, Mt. 24:27, with power and great glory, Mt. 24:30, at the time of cosmic catastrophes, Mt. 24:29, this is happening at the very end.

THEREFORE, BE HOLY

Because of the awesome glory and holiness of Jesus and the judgment at His coming, Peter warns the church to walk in holiness and to "be diligent to be found by him without spot or blemish, and at peace." 2 Pet. 3:11-14.

Time and again when Paul writes about this day of the coming of the Lord, the coming of Jesus, the day of judgment, he urges the church to the same blameless holy walk. "And it is my prayer that your love may abound more and more, with knowledge and all discernment, so that you may approve what is excellent, and so be pure and blameless for the day of Christ." Phil. 1:9, 10.

"And I am sure of this, that he who began a good work in you will bring it to completion at the day of Jesus Christ." Phil. 1:6.

"…so that you are not lacking in any gift, as you wait for the revealing of our Lord Jesus Christ, who will sustain you to the end, guiltless in the day of our Lord Jesus Christ." 1 Cor. 1:7, 8.

"…so that he may establish your hearts blameless in holiness before our God and Father, at the coming of our Lord Jesus with all his saints." 1 Thess. 3:13.

"Now may the God of peace himself sanctify you completely, and may your whole spirit and soul and body be kept blameless at the coming of our Lord Jesus Christ." 1 Thess. 5:23.

Accordingly, we must be holy, different from the world, separated unto service to God, unblemished and without blame, of use to God, living to honour His Name. Who is like that? Who is able? No one, no Christian, has his own sanctification in his hand. It is the work of the Holy Spirit to form us, to train and sanctify us. For that very purpose we must allow His working in us, we must surrender and entrust ourselves to Him. In this way He will sanctify us.

Peter and Paul urged us to be holy in connection with the coming of Jesus, His coming on that last day, when the earth will perish in fire. But also, in view of our own last day, the day when we pass away, and the Lord takes us home. The last day of world history might appear to be far off, but our own last day is always at hand, for a human life is but for a moment. So, make earnest with your own holiness. Therefore, be holy.

Paul also writes about that very last day in 1 Thess. 5:2; 1 Thess. 4:13-18; 2 Thess. 2:1-5, 8; Phil. 3:20, 21; 1 Cor. 15:50-55. The subject matter of these texts will be dealt with later in this Bible study.

REIGNING FROM HEAVEN

Because of His to human beings' unbearable holiness Jesus cannot physically and visibly present reign as King on earth. Jesus is too great for this earth. The earth would not be able to contain Him. If He would take place on a throne in Jerusalem, then once again He would have to humble and empty Himself and lay down His heavenly glory.

Jesus is enthroned in heaven, far above all power and authority, on the throne of God.

"So then the Lord Jesus, after he had spoken to them, was taken up into heaven and sat down at the right hand of God." Mk. 16:19.

"He is the radiance of the glory of God and the exact imprint of his nature, and he upholds the universe by the word of his power. After making purification for sins, he sat down at the right hand of the Majesty on high, having become as much superior to angels as the name he has inherited is more excellent than theirs." Hebr. 1:3, 4.

"…Jesus Christ, who has gone into heaven and is at the right hand of God, with angels, authorities, and powers having been subjected to him." 1 Pet. 3:22. Should the Lord now have to be seated on an earthly throne, then this would be a terrible indignity.

It is the Holy Spirit's work to convict concerning righteousness, because "I go to the Father, and you will see me no longer." John 16:10. It would be unrighteous if Jesus once again would have to leave the Father. This is not what He deserves.

HOW DOES JESUS REIGN? THROUGH THE SPIRIT!

Jesus Himself never depicted His kingship in this earthly manner, and He never raised the expectation that He would return in order to reign on earth.

He did say: "…it is to your advantage that I go away, for if I do not go away, the Helper will not come to you. But if I go, I will send him to you." John 16:7. Jesus thinks it is better for us, or more profitable, more to our advantage, that He is not physically present, but present in the Spirit with us. He reigns by His Spirit. Jesus reigns at the right hand of the Father in heaven, where He has received all power and authority, and His Spirit rules over the children of God.

From the Day of Pentecost on Jesus is King over all the earth, when the Spirit rested on each of the apostles, Acts 2:3. As judges or kings reside in their office, so the Spirit is enthroned on the children of God.

The kingship of Jesus is not of this earth, not according to the ways of this world. He reigns in a heavenly manner by the Spirit. It is better for the church that He judges in this manner.

HOW LONG WILL JESUS REIGN IN THIS WAY? UNTIL THE END OF THE AGE!

This form of reigning will not change. There will not come a time in our earthly history that He will be visibly present and enthroned somewhere on earth. Jesus says: "And I will ask the Father, and he will give you another Helper, to be with you forever." John 14:16. So, the Spirit will remain forever. The Spirit will not at some future moment exchange places with Jesus. Jesus, after bringing His one offer for sin, is forever seated at the right hand of God. Hebr. 10: 12, 13 says: "But when Christ had offered for all time a single sacrifice for sins, he sat down at the right hand of God, waiting from that time until his enemies should be made a footstool for his feet." The last enemy will be death, which will be overcome at the resurrection; 1 Cor. 15:25, 26.

Jesus told His disciples: "And behold, I am with you always, to the end of the age." Mt. 28:20. Until the end of the age Jesus is present with His church through the Holy Spirit, so this means not in a physical manner.

The church is a mission-church to the end of the age. People must come to faith on hearing, Rom. 10:11-15, and not just on seeing, for that would not require faith. Through faith we are saved. This is a rule valid from Adam until the last day. This rule counts for the Jew as well as for the Greek. This rule will never be changed.

JESUS' PROGRAM OF GOVERNING — EXECUTING GOD'S PLANS

Why did Jesus ascend into heaven? His ascension had a very important purpose, namely "that He might fill all things." Eph. 4:10.

To fill all things is to fulfil, or to bring to its destination, to carry out God's plan. At the right hand of God, the place of executing power, He brings the Gentiles to fullness, and will start to use them for the purpose for which He has called them: to be a people for God's Name and to be His witnesses, to provoke Israel to jealousy, Rom. 11:12, 25.

He also will bring Israel to fullness. Israel converted to her Messiah will be restored to her calling, the purpose for which they have been chosen: to be a blessing to all nations. In that manner He clearly will manifest His kingdom in all the world.

And only when the last, the seventh angel has sounded his trumpet, Rev. 10:7, will Jesus fulfil and accomplish every mystery of God, and every promise and every plan. Then the end of the age will be there. The definitive end of the 'things that can be shaken'. Hebr. 12:27. Then all will come to their destiny, to fullness. Then the preparation for the eternal kingdom is completed. The ascension of Jesus will serve for that purpose until that time.

The Church of all ages confesses to believe in Jesus that He is:

> "ascended into heaven,
> seated at the right hand of God,
> from where He will come to judge the living and the dead."

He is not coming to reign, for He already reigns at the right hand of God. He is coming to judge on the last day. After having dethroned all power and authority, He will hand over the Kingdom to the Father, so that God will be all in all, 1 Cor. 15:24-28.

HOW WILL WE UNDERSTAND THIS?

Don't the prophets speak of a messianic coming, so that the Kingdom of God will break through on the earth?

Certainly.

But the Scriptures that speak of *seeing* and *beholding*, of *coming* and *returning* within the framework of time and history must never be so literally understood that they contradict other Scriptures. The Lord does not contradict Himself in His own Word.

SEEING

We must understand *seeing* and *beholding* in the way that Jesus uses it in John 14:19, "Yet a little while and the world will see me no more, but you will see me. Because I live, you also will live." The disciples see Jesus, even when He has ascended into heaven. They see His work in the world. They see Him in the Spirit. This is also how the author of the letter to the Hebrews puts it: "…but we see Jesus." Hebr. 2:9

We are only able to see who the Son is if it has been revealed by the Father. The Father reveals the truth to the children concerning His Son, to those who are like little children; Lk. 10:21-24. Whoever is not born again or from above can't even see the kingdom of God; John 3:3. But we see the Kingdom, because we have been born again.

When Israel has turned back, they too shall see Jesus by the Holy Spirit. Then also it will be true for them what John writes: "For this is the will of my Father, that everyone who looks on the Son and believes in him should have eternal life." John 6:40.

When the Lord pours out over the house of David and Jerusalem the spirit of grace and supplication, Israel will understand and "look on Him, whom they have pierced." Zech. 12:10. Suddenly their blindness will be taken away and they will understand: He was pierced, so that His bones would not be broken. His bones were spared because He was the Lamb of God. YAHWEH saved the bones of His Passover Lamb!

Through the actions of God Israel will recognize the *identity* of their Messiah. They will *look* upon Him. "Your eyes will behold the king in his beauty." Isa. 33:17 and 22. Jesus will save them from their sins; Mt. 1:21. He will become for them "a fountain for cleansing from sin and uncleanness." Zech. 13:1. He also will deliver them from their enemies. So, a double salvation. Through His deeds they will see and recognise Jesus, as Moses also wrote in Dt. 11:7 "For your eyes have seen all the great work of the Lord that he did." David as well spoke of this in Psalm 63:2 "So I have looked upon you in the sanctuary, beholding your power and glory."

In faith Israel will call upon the Lord; Rom. 10:14. And they will see Him in faith. "For I tell you, you will not see me again, until you say, 'Blessed is he who comes in the name of the Lord.' " Mt. 23:39. Israel will not remain in unbelief. When she comes to faith Israel will be grafted back into her own olive tree; Rom. 11:23, 24. Israel, as all of us are asked to do, must also walk by faith and not by sight. 2 Cor. 5:7.

COMING

We must understand *coming* and *returning* as it is stated in Zech. 14:3 [KJV] where it says: "Then shall the Lord go forth, and fight against those nations, as when he fought in the day of battle." He will come *as when He fought in the day of battle!* How did He come in those days?

God *went out* to fight against Egypt. See the book of Exodus. God *came* to test Israel; Ex. 20:20.

But also: God *arose* to punish Israel; Isa. 28:21.

God *came* to deliver Israel from Babylon and was surprised about her unbelief; Isa. 50:2.

God *returned* to Zion when Israel was delivered from Babylon; Isa. 52:8.

This coming and returning of God was not in a physical way, but to the eye of faith it certainly was noticeable.

In Isaiah 28:21 we see the Lord acting, *as in former days*. "For the Lord will rise up as on Mount Perazim *(where the Lord broke through David's enemies before him)*; as in the Valley of Gibeon he will be roused; *(where in Joshua's days the Lord decided the battle against the Canaanites by throwing down huge hail stones)* to do his deed – strange is his deed! and to work his work – alien is his work!" *(italics mine)* Here the Lord threatens Israel, as in Zechariah 14 where He also brings Israel into distress. But in both these portions of Scripture the Lord has in view Israel's salvation. No actions where the Lord is visibly present, but certainly observable.

OBSERVABLY TAKING ACTION IN HISTORY

In this manner the Lord will return to again raise up the fallen hut of David; Acts 15:16. This will be a clearly observable, profound interaction of King Jesus! Through this action the Kingdom of God on earth will clearly be brought to the fore. But in this all, He Himself will not be visible.

Jesus will show Himself to be the Holy One of Israel, and act in sight of all the nations. And the nations, like Israel, will know that He is Lord. This word 'knowing' is used many times in the book of Ezekiel and has the same meaning as the word 'seeing' as used in Isaiah and Zechariah. Israel will *know*, will perceive and understand; Ezek. 20:41-44; Ezek. 37:6, 14. And the nations will *know* and understand that He is Lord; Ezek. 36:36; Ezek. 37:28.

This will happen when Israel turns back. "Come, let us return to the Lord! (…) he will come to us as the showers, as the spring rains that water the earth." Hos. 6:1-3. Then in the Spirit He comes to them.

INDWELLING

Every intervention of God to set things straight is meant for Him to dwell in the midst of His people; Ezek. 37:27; Zech. 2:10.

When He sent His Son into the world, Jesus says: "If anyone loves me, he will keep my word, and my Father will love him, and we will come to him and *make our home with him*." John 14:23.

When all of Israel embraces Jesus, He will fulfil that varied promise for them: "I will put my Spirit within you," Ezek. 36:27; Ezek. 37:14; Ezek. 39:29; Isa. 44:3; Joel 2:28, 29; Isa. 32:15; Zech. 12:10, so as to dwell and be always with them.

WORDS OF FIRE

When Israel awaits the coming of the Messiah, then this is with great fear and awe for His holiness, which the prophets also described in fiery terms. "For behold, the Lord will come in fire, and his chariots like the whirlwind, to render his anger in fury, and his rebuke with flames of fire." Isa. 66:15. The intervention of God in the midst of history will also be very formidable! A day of judgment is expected at the *coming* of the Messiah, a release of God's wrath.

"But who can endure the day of his coming, and who can stand when he appears? For he is like a refiner's fire and like fullers' soap." Mal. 3:2. Israel will be cleansed with the fire of the Holy Spirit, purifying them as gold and silver. Isaiah too uses the metaphor of a goldsmith, Isa. 1:25, 26, depicting how Israel is once again restored to be a holy nation: "I will turn my hand against you and will smelt away your dross as with lye and remove all your alloy. And I will restore your judges as at the first, and your counselors as at the beginning." Zechariah as well uses the picture of the forge in Zech. 13:9.

"For behold, the day is coming, burning like an oven." Mal. 4:1. The evildoers and the arrogant are like 'stubble' and will be 'set ablaze'. They will be exposed by the Holy Spirit and humbled to being nobodies, so that those who fear the Name of God will be put in the right. They will tread down the wicked under the soles of their feet, Mal. 4:3, as also Satan is crushed beneath our feet because of the victory of Jesus; Rom. 16:20.

"But for you who fear my name, the sun of righteousness shall rise…" A new day, a day of salvation, will dawn after that very great distress, after that fearful cleansing, after Israel – and Christianity not excepted – is restored and fire-refined into a royal priesthood; Mal. 3.

On the Isle of Patmos John sees the sun of a new day dawning because of the action of 'the other angel', whose face is like the sun; Rev. 10:1. Here as well it goes through a fiery judgment. The legs and feet of the angel are like pillars of fire and he set them on the sea and on the land. Through this terrifying, fiery, spiritual judgment humanity worldwide is requisitioned, is taken possession of.

The Lord is a jealous God; Exo. 34:14. His jealousy is a consuming fire, "For the Lord your God is a consuming fire, a jealous God." Dt. 4:24. And because of this envy, this all-consuming jealousy, He will provoke Israel to jealousy by the working of the Holy Spirit, in order that Israel once again will return to Him.

In our time and history Jesus will intervene in a holy, awe-inspiring and convincing manner. The Holy Spirit will glorify Him; John 16:14. For this to happen He does not have to be physically present.

THE LOVE OF JESUS

ALL SHALL KNOW HIM

Jesus said: "It is better for you…" that He would not physically remain on earth to reign, but that He would do this through the presence and working of the Holy Spirit. In this manner Jesus lovingly protects us from Himself.

When scoffers ask about the long-delayed coming of Jesus, Peter points to the longsuffering of the Lord: "The Lord is not slow to fulfil his promise as some count slowness, but is patient toward you, not wishing that any should perish, but that all should reach repentance." 2 Pet. 3:9. Jesus so loves the world that He does not desire that any would perish. If He would return today, many would be lost.

There are over a billion Chinese people in this world who do not know Jesus, and there are five hundred million inhabitants in India who have never heard of Jesus. And many millions of people living in the Eastern Bloc nations, who but only today are able to hear of the love and mercy of Jesus. (The author wrote this before the fall of the Iron Curtain – *Translator's note*)

If Jesus would come today, then all these would perish because of His holiness. Jesus first gives the whole world a chance to get to know Him.

When Jesus Himself speaks about His coming, He says that the gospel must be proclaimed throughout the whole world as a testimony to all nations; Mt. 24:14. Only then the end will come with His return; Mt. 24:27, 30.

The Old Testament tells us that there will come a time when every knee shall bow to the Lord and every tongue shall confess His Name; Isa. 45:23.

Even though God threatens with the great and awesome day of the Lord, yet from the last text in the Old Testament we learn that the Lord *does not desire to come* to strike the earth with a curse; Mal. 4:5, 6. This is because of His great love and mercy. His love will first bring about an 'elianic action' and provide for a renewal and restoration.

His love will first reclaim the world. First, salvation by way of the Servant of the Lord will reach to the ends of the earth; Isa. 49:6. God will act in such a manner that there will be peace over all the earth and all will know Him. God will create a new heaven and earth, i.e. a renewed heaven and a renewed earth, a kingdom of peace; Isa. 65:17-25, as a foreshadowing of the new heaven and earth in the eternal kingdom about which both Peter and John spoke; 2 Peter 3:13; Rev. 21.

In this temporal kingdom of Isa. 65, with the renewed heaven and renewed earth, the earth will be filled with the knowledge of the Lord, Isa. 11:9b, Hab. 2:14, as the waters cover the sea. Isa. 65:17-25 speaks about the same time as Isa. 11; compare Isa. 65:25 with Isa. 11:6 and 9a.

All nations will seek Jesus, the root of Jesse, Isa. 11:10, and will receive instruction from Zion, from where God's law and justice will go forth; Isa. 2:3. Chinese, Russians, Buddhists, Muslims, all will then know Him.

Because of His love Jesus will only come after the millennial kingdom of peace, after all will have had a chance to get to know Him and come to repentance. He will come when once again apostasy will have returned. His coming carries with it judgment and the ungodly, who will be overtaken by this judgment, will in the end be responsible for it themselves and will not have an excuse. They will have heard of and been acquainted with Jesus and will again have rejected Him.

CHANGE

However, the love of Jesus has a protecting measure against His fiery holiness for all those who have remained in Him; as citizens of the heavenly kingdom, all those who looked for the eternal kingdom. "For God has not destined us for wrath, but to obtain salvation through our Lord Jesus Christ." 1 Thess. 5:9.

Our mortal bodies will not be able to endure His appearing. But Paul explains that our mortal bodies will be changed; Phil. 3:20, 21 "But our citizenship is in heaven, and from it we await a Savior, the Lord Jesus Christ, who will *transform* our lowly body to be like his glorious body, by the power that enables him even to subject all things to himself."

In 1 Cor. 15:50-55 Paul tells us that we all will be changed at the last trumpet: "For this perishable body must put on the imperishable, and this mortal body must put on immortality," verse 53, just as those who have died in Christ will be raised imperishable at His coming on that same day; 1 Cor. 15:52. Then the last enemy, death, will have been totally overcome, 1 Cor. 15:54, and so also put beneath the feet of Jesus; Heb.10:13. Then Jesus will deliver the kingdom to God the Father, so that God will be all in all; 1 Cor. 15:23 and 24-28. This is the ultimate goal.

RAISED UP ON THE LAST DAY

When Jesus speaks about the resurrection, He also says repeatedly, up to four times, that this will take place on the last day of world history. "And this is the will of him who sent me, that I should lose nothing of all that he has given me, but raise it up on the last day." John 6:39.

"For this is the will of my Father, that everyone who looks on the Son and believes in him should have eternal life, and I will raise him up on the last day." John 6:40. And in verse 44 Jesus continues: "No one can come to me unless the Father who sent me draws him. And I will raise him up on the last day." And likewise, in verse 54: "Whoever feeds on my flesh and drinks my blood has eternal life, and I will raise him up on the last day."

THE RAPTURE

As in 1 Cor. 15:50-55, Paul also writes about this in his first letter to the Thessalonians, 1 Thess. 4:13-18, how that at the sound of the trumpet first the dead in Christ will rise. "Then we who are alive, who are left, will be caught up together with them in the clouds *(in the twinkling of an eye – 1 Cor. 15:52)* to meet the Lord in the air, and so we will always be with the Lord." Then all those who have died **and** all those still living at this time will together meet the Lord in the air. This is what is generally known as the 'rapture'. So, the rapture occurs on the same last day of history.

In John 14:2, 3 Jesus also spoke about this being caught up: "In my Father's house are many rooms. If it were not so, would I have told you that I go to prepare a place for you? And if I go and prepare a place for you, I will come again and will take you to myself, that where I am you may be also."

When Paul writes about the 'rapture', or about being caught up, meeting the Lord in the air, 1 Thess. 4:17, or about "our being gathered together to him," 2 Thess. 2:1, then he states that the dead will rise first on the day of the sounding of the trumpet of God, 1 Thess. 4:16, and that this day is also the day of the last trumpet when we are changed, 1 Cor. 15:52, the last day, as Jesus calls it — John 6:39.

So, the return of the Lord, our being changed, raised and being caught up all take place on the last day, the day that the world will be judged and will pass away by fire. This will take place after the millennial kingdom of peace, after that all will have had a chance to know Jesus.

EVIDENCE OF JESUS' LOVE

The love of Jesus keeps Him from coming before the millennium, before that all will have had a chance to know Him, so that not many millions will unknowingly perish.

The love of Jesus protects His children from His holiness by giving them a changed body and so taking them, along with those raised, to Himself.

The love of Jesus also makes His church know the time of His coming through prophecy and through recognizing the signs which He will give.

WHEN DOES JESUS COME?

Are we able to know when the day of Christ will be? Can we know the day of His coming?

Yes and No.

NO. Peter says that that day "will come like a thief," 2 Pet. 3:10. Paul too says that that day comes "like a thief in the night." 1 Thess. 5:2. And Jesus says: "But concerning that day and hour no one knows, not even the angels of heaven, nor the Son, but the Father only." Mt. 24:36. He compares the unexpected and suddenness of that day with the time of Noah, Mt. 24:37-39. "Therefore, stay awake, for you do not know on what day your Lord is coming," verse 42.

YES. Yet the church at that time will roughly know the time of His coming. Noah knew from God's instructions exactly when he had to go into the ark. The godless and the unbelieving were the ones who suddenly were overtaken by the flood. The believers are not in darkness, for that day to surprise them like a thief; 1 Thess. 5:4. The two witnesses of the last days, Rev. 11:3, will certainly be allowed to prophetically announce that day, for the Lord does not do anything without declaring it to His servants, the prophets, Amos 3:7. The call of a prophet, of a herald, will sound: "Here is the bridegroom! Come out to meet him." Mt. 25:6.

Furthermore, signs have been given announcing that day. Jesus admonishes us to pay attention to the signs of the times.

SIGNS GIVEN

Jesus points to signs of His coming:

- The abomination of desolation, Mt. 24:15, along with the great tribulation; Mt. 24:9, 21.

- Immediately after this the shaking of the powers of heaven, the darkening of the sun and the moon and the falling of the stars from heaven; Mt. 24:29. The cosmic catastrophes.

Both these signs agree with the fifth and sixth seal from Revelation 6. This chapter gives in a nutshell the flow of history from the time of Jesus to the day of His return, "the great day of their wrath" and "who can stand?" Rev. 6:17. The first four seals form a unity and refer to the time before the millennial kingdom of peace. They are comparable to the beginning of the birth pains as described in Mt. 24:4-8, but "the end is not yet." Mt. 24:6.

The word 'then' in verse 9 points to another time, the time of apostasy after the kingdom of peace. This 'then' we also see in verse 14. It indicates the last events on earth at the end of our time and history, after all nations have been acquainted with the gospel.

- The abomination of desolation and the great tribulation, Mt. 24:15, 21, are the same as the fifth seal: the souls under the altar must wait for a short time for the martyrs of the great tribulation; Rev. 6:9-11.

- The cosmic catastrophes, the shaking of the powers of heaven, Mt. 24:29, are mentioned in the sixth seal: "the sun became black as sackcloth, the full moon became like blood, and the stars of the sky fell to the earth as the fig tree sheds its winter fruit when shaken by a gale. The sky vanished like a scroll that is being rolled up." Rev. 6:12-17. This ancient, perishable creation is undone.

This final judgment is God's answer to the apostasy after the kingdom of peace and Satan's last attack on the children of God.

Paul as well describes the first sign given by Jesus to which the believers must pay attention. "Let no one deceive you in any way. For that day will not come, unless the rebellion comes first, and the man of lawlessness is revealed, the son of destruction, who opposes and exalts himself against every so-called god or object of worship, so that he takes his seat in the temple of God, proclaiming himself to be God." 2 Thess. 2:3, 4.

The son of perdition, the man of lawlessness, is the beast rising out of the sea in Revelation 13, whom the whole earth follows after and marvels at and worships, who speaks haughty and blasphemous words.

This son of perdition, who is worshipped in the temple as a god, is also the Antichrist as mentioned in Daniel 11:30, who is enraged and takes action against the holy covenant and profanes the temple and sets up the abomination that makes desolate; Dan. 13:31; 12:11; 9:27; Mt. 24:15.

The abomination that makes desolate is the image of the beast rising out of the sea, Rev. 13:14b, that speaks and marks, and that kills; Rev. 13:15, 16.

It is good for us to once more listen carefully to what Paul says in 2 Thess. 2:1-4, "Now concerning the coming of our Lord Jesus Christ and our being gathered together to him, we ask you, brothers, not to be quickly shaken in mind or alarmed, either by a spirit or a spoken word, or a letter seeming to be from us, to the effect that the day of the Lord has come. Let no one deceive you in any way. For that day will not come, unless the rebellion comes first, and the man of lawlessness is revealed, the son of destruction, who opposes and exalts himself against every so-called god or object of worship, so that he takes his seat in the temple of God, proclaiming himself to be God." And in 2 Thess. 2:8, "…whom the Lord Jesus will kill with the breath of his mouth and bring to nothing by the appearance of his coming."

So first the rebellion and the tribulation under the lawless one, then the coming of Jesus with the cosmic catastrophes and the judgment of the Antichrist. "Now when these things begin to take place, straighten up and raise your heads, because your redemption is drawing near." Lk. 21:28.

THE TEMPLE

When the Antichrist sets himself in the temple of God then this is the beginning of the end. But for this to happen the temple of God must first be raised up. Not the stone building in Jerusalem. That temple service was fulfilled in Christ Jesus. When Israel, in her rejection of the fulfilment of the shadow service, continued to worship at the Temple, God, forty years after the first appearing of the Lamb of God, allowed this Temple to be destroyed by Titus in AD 70. The blood sacrifices were no longer needed. Today the Lord builds a spiritual house, a dwelling place of God in the Spirit, the Church of Jew and Gentile together. Jesus says that He will raise His temple on the third day, His own resurrection being the guarantee of this.

Revelation 11:1 also shows us that there will be a recognizable, manifest and measurable temple of the Lord, the church, whose outer court afterwards will be trodden down in the time of the Antichrist; Rev. 11:2. Therefore, before the rebellion comes, there must first come a restoration. A restoration that can only be realized in the kingdom of peace, the millennium. For today the church, God's temple, is still totally divided.

A spiritual house does not necessarily exclude a stone building. It is possible that in Jerusalem there will be a church, a conference building, or a theological seminary/university. Not a temple in which the old-testamentical worship service will have been restored, but maybe a place where Jesus' sacrifice for the forgiveness of our sins is preached.

KEPT FROM DECEPTION

The love of Jesus directs us to the signs. Furthermore, He Himself takes care that His children will recognize these signs, that they will be kept from the deception of the Antichrist. "And none of the wicked shall understand, but those who are wise shall understand." Dan. 12:10. "And the wise among the people shall make many understand." Dan. 11:33. "For you are all children of light, children of the day. We are not of the night or of the darkness." 1 Thess. 5:5. "For false christs and false prophets will arise and perform great signs and wonders, so as to lead astray, if possible, even the elect." Mt. 24:24. But this is not possible, for Jesus keeps them from the evil one in the hour of deception. "But the Lord is faithful. He will establish you and guard you against the evil one." 2 Thess. 3:3. In John 17:15 Jesus prayed: "I do not ask that you take them out of the world," – so no rapture in the midst of time and history or before the great tribulation – "but that you keep them from the evil one."

"Because you have kept my word about patient endurance, I will keep you from the hour of trial that is coming on the whole world, to try those who dwell on the earth." Rev. 3:10.

Apparently, at that time there will be something in the world that can be tempted and tested, namely *faith*. Not: *beholding and knowing*. The whole world will then have believed, will have become acquainted with the Gospel; Mt. 24:14. Those who faithfully have kept expecting the coming of Jesus, will be kept from stumbling or defeat.

The love of Christ will help the believer, keeping him from the evil one and his temptation in this time of distress.

THE SHORT TIME

The love of Jesus also will cause those days to be cut short for the sake of the elect, Mt. 24:22, then the persecuted church will be taken up.

Daniel 12:1 also describes how His people will be delivered in a time of trouble as there has never been before since the nations have existed – see also Mt. 24:21 – "But at that time your people shall be delivered *(through the Rapture)*, everyone whose name shall be found written in the book." Daniel 12:2 says: "And many of those who sleep in the dust of the earth shall awake." Thus, Daniel also sees in that time the great tribulation as well as the escape *(the rapture)* and the resurrection. Daniel himself as well will arise at the end of days; Dan. 12:13.

So, Jesus does not come before but during the great tribulation, in order to save His people from this unimaginable great distress; Phil. 3:20; Lk. 21:28.

John too in the book of Revelation mentions again and again the cutting short of the time of tribulation, every time when he speaks about Satan's last offense, his last attack on the children of God by means of the beasts from the sea and from the earth. See for example Rev. 6:11, where the souls of the martyrs had to rest a little longer; or Rev. 17:10, where the beast would only remain a little while; or Rev. 20:3, where, after the kingdom of peace, the serpent had to be released from the pit for a little while.

When it concerns that short time, expressions are used such as 'forty-two months', Rev.11:2, or 'twelve hundred and sixty days', Rev. 11:3 and

12:6, or 'three and a half days', Rev. 11:9, or 'time, times and half a time', Rev. 12:14; Dan. 7:25; Dan. 12:7.

'Half a day' or 'half a time' points to the half-way cutting off of Satan's work and plans. Satan never will succeed in arriving at his goal.

Continually the 'short' or 'half a time' is about that same, intense period of history which will be cut short because of Jesus' love. He has put a merciful limit to that.

The value of Jesus' sacrificial blood

Not yet

From the writings of the Apostles and the words of Jesus, His coming will mean the end of the world as we know it, and furthermore, it will mark the beginning of the eternal kingdom.

Should we expect this end of the ages shortly?

- There is not yet unity between followers of Christ from Jew and Gentile, so there is not yet a restored temple.

- There has also been no kingdom of peace, where all nations will have learned Christ.

- There hasn't been an antichristian world ruler, let alone one who allows himself to be worshipped as a god.

- The church is not yet persecuted worldwide, because of their refusal to worship that lawless one. So, the great tribulation of the last days is definitely not here yet.

When I consider the worth of Jesus' blood, I can hardly imagine a soon coming **and** ending of the world. I am not satisfied with getting one pound of salt for a thousand dollars. I expect more value for my money!

Enough for all

For the offer of Jesus, the Son of God – and not just a man – we should not be satisfied with the small percentage of born-again Christians found in the world today. The blood of Jesus should yield tremendously more than that. He could redeem the whole world with it. This is how John the Baptist introduced Jesus as the Lamb of God, who takes away the sin of the world; John 1:29.

The blood of Jesus is so costly and so valuable that God will get all that He can out of it. First the whole world will get a magnanimous, abundantly clear and convincing chance to repent. The angels sang "peace on earth" because of the certainty of the victory! Jesus not only gave His life for the individual soul. He died for whole nations, yes, for the whole world.

FOR ISRAEL …

In the first place for Israel. That is what the angel said to Joseph: "…for he will save his people from their sins." Mt. 1:21. The angel brought the good news of great joy to the shepherds that would be *for all the people* (Israel); Lk. 2:10. This is also what Jesus said to the Canaanite woman: "I was sent only to the lost sheep of the house of Israel." Mt. 15:24.

Peter expressed himself in similar vein to the men of Israel: "God, having raised up his servant, sent him to you first, to bless you by turning every one of you from your wickedness." Acts 3:26.

When Jesus builds His spiritual temple, Israel certainly will not be missing. All of Israel will come to her destiny thanks to the blood of Jesus.

… AND FOR THE NATIONS

Jesus also died for the other nations, for Arabs, Africans, Chinese, et cetera. That is why God gave Him a Name above every other name, so that at the name of Jesus *every knee* should bow, and *every tongue* confess that Jesus is Lord, to the glory of God the Father; Phil. 2:9-11. His salvation is for all. Not only will He sanctify His people Israel by His blood, Hebr. 13:12, but also us. We also have come near because of His blood, come into a relationship with Him; Eph. 2:13. He ransomed them from every tribe and language and people and nation for God to make them a royal priesthood; Rev. 5:9, 10.

The gospel of the cross will reach the ends of the world, for the forgiveness of sin is for all nations; Lk. 24:27; Mk. 16:15; Mt. 28:19 and Mt. 24:14. Through the blood of Jesus all things will be reconciled to God; Col. 1:20. As long as the whole world has not yet heard the offer of grace through the blood of Jesus, the end of the age will and must not yet dawn.

THE POWER TO OVERCOME

The whole Bible describes the war annals of God. In it the battles of the Lord are recorded. In Gen. 3:15 God declares war on Satan and in Revelation God reveals to John how the battle will be won and how this outcome, already proclaimed in Genesis, the victory over Satan, will be realized.

These two battling armies are called the seed of the woman and the seed of the serpent. That is, those who in trust let themselves be used by God, over against those who outside of God, knowingly or not, are used by Satan. In Revelation 12 John sees this battle from the earliest days of human history to the last day. The child Jesus was taken up into heaven; Rev. 12:5 and Acts 1:9.

The woman, the church of the old and new covenant, remains in the battle until the definitive victory. Before Satan starts his last and most fierce offense against the "rest of her offspring" in the great tribulation, John is shown, as comfort for the community of the last days, how Satan has already been defeated in heaven and therefore also will suffer defeat here on earth. He also is allowed to see how Satan is overcome: "by the blood of the Lamb and by the word of their testimony, for they loved not their lives even unto death." The seed of the woman, God's battle army, wages war by the blood of Jesus. His blood is *the* weapon of victory. The gospel of the cross is the power that Satan is not able to overcome.

As good soldiers they don't fear the battle, they are not afraid to die, they are even willing to give their lives for the cause of their Lord. Every victory over Satan is a victory from out of the suffering of Jesus.

BINDING THROUGH THE POWER OF JESUS' BLOOD

Satan will be bound before the Millennium; Rev. 20:2. This binding will also be the result of Jesus' sacrificial offer on the cross.

Through united faith in the blood of the Passover Lamb, through the united proclamation of Jesus' death at the Lord's Table – by which the unity of the church will be restored, temple restoration! – Satan will be made powerless. When believers allow themselves to be linked into a strong chain on the basis of the blood of Jesus, then, in that unity, Satan will be fettered and bound. Satan will never be overcome by the struggle of many small ecclesiastical armies who operate on their own without any unity. How then will peace come about? When all believers together form one front line through the restoration of the divided Lord's Supper Table, then Satan will and must lose. For it is there that the Lord will give His Spirit power. This is how Christ will be glorified.

Through the proclamation of Jesus' death all power of hell will be defeated. Through the blood of Jesus God will expose the modern, liberal biblical criticism, the false ecumenism in our churches. And by that same blood God will dethrone the hierarchical power and dogma of good works in the Roman Catholic church, when He demonstrates the authority of the Spirit and confirms it by grace alone. It will heal the hardening and blindness of Israel, when the Lord, on the united confession of the blood of the Lamb, sends His spiritual fire, by which Israel will be convicted that Jesus after all is their Messiah. This will be the answer to antichristian, secular Zionism. The aggressively positioned Islam will shrink back from the blood of Jesus. Every Eastern religion will be overcome. And worldly ideologies such as communism and neofascism will disappear because of the power of the gospel of the cross. Every demonic, antichristian power will be defeated by the unmeasurable, overwhelming power of Jesus' blood. And in all this Jesus will be glorified. His supremacy will be apparent.

UNITY IS NEEDED

We should not think too small about the divine offer of God's Son! We must not expect too little (not just our individual salvation) of God's merciful offer on Golgotha! We must not underestimate the power of the blood of Jesus.

As long as the body of the Lord remains divided, it remains powerless. As soon as the believers humbly come together around the blood of reconciliation, there will be grace for the churches, restoration and power to fight and overcome.

Jesus expects that God's love and His mission will become evident in the unity of the church. In John 17:23 He prays "that they may become perfectly one, so that the world may know that you sent me and loved them even as you loved me." Our division will never bring the world to the acknowledgement of God's love manifested in Christ. Jesus wants our unity.

To bind Satan, a massive offensive is needed against him. God's army will have to pull together and form one front. On our collective confession of faith in Jesus' sacrifice the Lord will bind the devil by His angel. Then the millennial kingdom of peace will break through, that which we all long for.

THE LAST OFFENSIVE

After the Millennium Satan is loosed once again; Rev. 20:7. Alas, faith will wane. There will be people in the later generations that will not know of thankfulness for Jesus' sacrifice. The gospel of the cross will then be abandoned or changed.

Links will be broken in the chain and the lid of the pit will crack open. Consequently, because of our unfaithfulness and negligence, Satan will once again get a chance for his last offense. There is also a holy 'must' in this opportunity, so that the thoughts of our hearts will be revealed. It is like a test case.

Satan's last offensive is recorded in Rev. 20:8; Rev. 19:19; Rev. 17:4; Rev. 13:7 and Rev. 12:17, and what are the consequences for the true church is recorded in Rev. 6:11; Rev. 11:7; Rev. 13:17. It will be a climax in persecution and oppression, a climax in martyrdom; Mt. 24:21; Dan. 12:1.

IMITATION

Revelation 13 describes how Satan organizes his last offensive, namely by way of his two instruments, to wit the beast rising from the sea (a political figure, a world leader) and his prophet, the beast rising from the earth (a religious power). Satan will act as the great imitator of the gospel. He imitates the Trinity of God, for he presents himself as God. The beast from the sea presents himself as the Christ, the King of the world. The beast from the earth acts as instrument of the Holy Spirit, as the prophet who points to the false christ, calling for the worship of his image.

Satan also imitates the resurrection of Jesus, by making the beast from the sea recover from a mortal wound. The beast from the earth disguises himself with the horns as of a lamb. He places a false gospel over against the biblical gospel, distorting the Bible and its witness.

Revelation emphasizes this imitation with expressions such as: "Who is like the beast?" – Rev. 13:4, over against the name of Michael in Rev. 12:7, which means: 'who is like God?' Also by putting a mark on the hand or the forehead, over against the sealing on the forehead as recorded in Rev. 7:3. Moreover, the appellation "that was, and is not, and is about to rise," in Rev. 17:8 over against the Name of God "who is and who was and who is to come," in Rev. 1:4, 8 and Rev. 4:8. With this God warns us that the imitation and counterfeiting is very subtle and cunning.

When Satan uses the gospel in such a subtle manner, then all who are not born again will be misled. All the more because the beast from the sea and the beast from the earth certainly will be very attractive, engaging and brilliant. The whole earth will follow them to the amazement of all. However, in God's sight they are beastly.

DISCERNING RECOGNITION

All those who entertain the wrong assumption that Jesus will reign bodily on the earth, will identify the beast rising from the sea as Christ. Their faulty expectation will pave the way for the antichrist.

However, those that know that Jesus' holiness never can be enthroned on earth in a bodily manner, but that He reigns through the Holy Spirit, will, after the warning of Jesus, not seek any place on earth where He might be; Mt. 24:23-26. They expect Him with great power and glory from heaven. True believers, warned by the Holy Spirit, will recognize as carnal a Christ-like figure who sets himself up as world ruler on a throne in Jerusalem. Whoever, as a citizen of the kingdom of heaven, continues to hold on to his or her salvation by the blood of Jesus, will be led by the Spirit in all truth and kept from this insidious temptation. The issue is to stay in fellowship with Jesus.

FAITHFUL UNTO DEATH

If they do not worship the image of the beast, they will be starved and beheaded, or persecuted and killed in different ways.

The true believers will continue to remember the Lord's death *until He comes*; 1 Cor. 11:26. Because of their faith in Jesus' offer on the cross the Lord will shorten that time, rescue them and take them up into heaven.

Satan will be overcome by the blood of the Lamb and by the fact that they do not love their lives even unto death. Satan can orchestrate some very smart war strategies, but his definitive defeat is certain. At the coming of the Lord of lords and the King of kings the lawless one and his prophet and their lord Satan will be cast into the lake of fire that burns with sulphur. Jesus conquers as the Lamb of God; Rev. 17:14.

THE END OF THE AGE

Then the end of the age will be there. The end of the age, the consummation of all things, will mean the completion of the preparation for God's new creation, the new humanity in the eternal kingdom, where righteousness dwells and God will be all in all.

After the definitive victory over Satan the earth will pass away. However, a new heaven and a new earth will then be ready, Rev. 21:1, the eternal kingdom for all God's blood-bought children. This eternal kingdom is the greatest and most valuable fruit of Jesus' sacrifice.

OUR TIME

Our time knows of much lawlessness and lukewarmness, the turning away from God, waning faith and antichristian ideologies. But it is not yet the time of the apostasy of the last days. It is a foreshadowing or prelude of it. Yet it is a time of strengthening the weak hands and straitening the shaking knees. It is especially in this time that when Jesus is no longer acknowledged as the Son of God and many condescendingly dispose of the Gospel of the cross as old fashioned, and by and large our human efforts have not produced much hope for peace, that we have once again to become battle ready and radically consider our greatest weapon: the blood of the Lamb, God's Son, and the Word of God. But we must use this weapon in unison, in one accord. The victory over all opposition is certain. Upon this united acknowledgment of His blood Jesus will give the power of His Holy Spirit, power to convict, and the binding of Satan. Jesus will give peace.

Satan will not just let himself be bound. He certainly will resist. But all those who long for the glorification of Jesus will not allow themselves to be discouraged by his threatenings. Whoever follows Jesus must take up his cross. "And whoever does not take his cross and follow me is not worthy of me." Mt. 10:38. The great decisions and turnings in history fall in difficult times. But the opposition as seen in our days is but a hint of the great tribulation of the last days.

As in the past, in the days of the Old Testament, Jesus will come in the Spirit, invisible, in order to manifest His supremacy. He will glorify Himself and deliver us from all present-day powers hostile to Him. He will intervene in the history of the world to bring peace, but only on the basis of His shed blood.

We must expect much from the power of His blood. We should not be too sparingly with our expectations. The blood of Jesus will bring about a tremendous harvest and will deliver a great victory. Peace on earth, where all will learn to know Him.

Let us pray perseveringly for the unity of all believers around the blood of reconciliation. This is how the glory and power of Jesus is revealed.

Jesus and the Name of God

The Powerful Present One

Whoever wants to contemplate the biblical future, must pay attention to the Name of God, YHWH, I AM WHO I AM. God's Name is His essence, His character. God's Name is connected with His purpose, His plans. He is I AM WHO I AM, dynamically present. Because He is concerned with humanity He will always direct His actions to deliver them from the power of His great adversary. His goal is the salvation of the world.

God Makes Himself a Name

God has made a Name for Himself. He made a Name through His deeds. When Daniel, Nehemiah and Jeremiah in their prayers pleaded for Israel, they mentioned how God made Himself a Name by delivering Israel from Egypt; Jer. 32:20; Neh. 9:10; Dan. 9:15. Then they prayed if the Lord, for the sake of His Name, would once again turn Israel back and save them.

The God of Abraham, Isaac and Jacob

The Lord made His Name known first to Moses at the burning bush; Ex. 3:14. The Lord remembered His covenant promise to Abraham, Isaac and Jacob; Ex. 2:24. He wants to save the world by way of Israel. He wants Israel to become a blessing for the nations; Gen. 12:2; Gen. 22:18. Remembering this promise He delivered Israel out of Egypt by the power of the blood of the Passover lamb. I AM WHO I AM acting for salvation, with His plan in view, challenging opposing powers. The Lord connects His Name YHWH with the Name of the God of Abraham, Isaac and Jacob; Ex. 3:15, "This is my name forever, and thus I am to be remembered throughout all generations." God wants to be known forever as the God of Israel.

When He decisively acts, intervening in world history, then this is for the sake of His Name, which we never must divorce from Israel. For He is faithful. Faithful to His Name and therefore faithful to Israel, *and* faithful to the world which He wants to bless by way of Israel.

A Priestly Nation

When Israel is brought out of Egypt, God makes a covenant with them at Mt. Sinai. They have to be a priestly nation, a nation of mediators, because all the families of the earth belong to Him; Ex. 19:5, 6. The nations learn to know Him through His actions with Israel. In this way His Name is revealed among the nations. See for example Josh. 2:9-11 or 1 Sam. 4:8. In faithfulness He acts for the sake of His Name, even despite the unfaithfulness of Israel; Ez. 20:9, 14, 22 "But I acted for the sake of my name, that it should not be profaned in the sight of the nations among whom they lived, in whose sight I made myself known to them in bringing them out of the land of Egypt." Time and again He delivered and restored Israel for the sake of His Name; Ez. 20:44; Ez. 36:22-27. This is how God sanctifies His Name; Ez. 39:7, 25.

JESUS

The name of Jesus stands for YHWH saves. I AM WHO I AM saves through Jesus. The Lord Jesus is the executor of God's plans. He is going to save. In the first place He wants to save Israel from their sins, Mt. 1:21; Acts 3:25, 26, but also others. He is the Lamb of God who takes away the sin of the world; John 1:29. Through the blood of the Passover Lamb there is deliverance from the power of Satan. Through the blood there will be the judgment of Satan and of all those who are on his side.

As a priestly nation Israel had to offer Jesus, according to the predetermined counsel of God, Acts 2:23, but they too by receiving Him could have received forgiveness; Acts 2:38. Alas, the majority of Israel has rejected Him. But their rejection of Jesus became a blessing for the Gentiles; Rom. 11:11. However, Paul expects that their acceptance of Jesus will yet bring about a much greater blessing for the world; Rom. 11:12, 15. Then once again they will be a priestly nation, Isa. 61:6, a nation of mediators, and will bless the world as crown witnesses of the Lamb of God. Isa. 43:21, "…the people whom I formed for myself that they might declare my praise."

A PEOPLE FOR HIS NAME

When the apostles were confused concerning the inclusion of the Gentiles into the new covenant in Christ Jesus, they came to the understanding that now the Lord specifically was going to give precedence to the Gentiles in faithfulness to His Name, so that after that and through their inclusion Israel would once again be restored. At the apostolic council in Jerusalem it was posited that God was going to take a people for His Name from the Gentiles, Acts 15:14, that He was going to use this people to restore Israel to Himself. God's Name is sanctified when we, Gentiles, function towards the conversion of Israel, towards Israel's acceptance of Jesus, and Israel's restoration to her calling to be a nation of mediators, of priests. Isn't this what Jesus wants us to pray: "Hallowed be Your Name"?

Before Paul set out in Romans chapters 9 to 11 God's way with Israel by way of the Gentiles, he stated in chapter 1 that he was set apart to bring about the obedience of faith for the sake of His Name among all the nations. Furthermore, God's actions with the Gentiles, His involvement with them, has to provoke Israel to jealousy, Rom. 11:11, so that the Jewish people also will long for God, who in Christ Jesus has revealed Himself as Saviour.

OUR GENTILE CHRISTIAN CALLING

God is going to involve and use the Gentile Christian church to restore Israel. Paul explains in Romans 11 how we are to function for God's Name, or how we can be used in the conversion and restoration of Israel. "...through their trespass salvation has come to the Gentiles, so as to make Israel jealous;" Rom. 11:11. We have to arouse their jealousy and their longing for Christ's deliverance.

"So they too have now been disobedient in order that by the mercy shown to you they also may now receive mercy." Rom. 11:31, 33. God's mercy shown to us must become instrumental in becoming God's mercy to Israel. It will be God's jealousy-provoking actions of grace and mercy towards us which will in the end draw Israel back to God. It doesn't concern just a few from Israel, but it concerns the whole nation; Rom. 11:25, 26 "a partial hardening has come upon Israel, until the fullness of the Gentiles has come in. And in this way all Israel will be saved."

FULLNESS

The fullness of the Gentiles will come in. However, a fullness can only occur when there is a void. The Gentile Christian community has nothing to offer to God, they have empty hands, on many points they are guilty before God, they are divided and lost, they have become arrogant towards Israel and have become the cause of much of Israel's suffering through the ages. When this community confesses its guilt, and humbles itself before God, pleading on the finished work of Christ, then in their emptiness He graciously will give His fullness, so that Israel will be saved. His Name will be hallowed!

I AM is present and actively at work and for the sake of Israel's turning back and salvation He will fill a restored and humbled Gentile Christian church with His power, with His Spirit, with His mercy, with His grace and gifts, with His secrets, so that Israel will be provoked to jealousy. Only in this way will the Gentiles function for God's Name.

To come to fullness, or the coming in of the fullness, really means the coming to the promised purpose of God. Fullness means: God acting in fulfilment. The Spirit at work in the church will convict Israel; John 16:8-11.

POWER NEEDED

Jesus too explained that the church needs power for the restoration of the kingdom to Israel; Acts 1:8. The disciples asked: "Lord, will you at this time restore the kingdom to Israel?" Jesus told them that they did not needed to know the when and the how of this restoration, but that in the first place they needed to receive power towards this. "But you will receive power when the Holy Spirit has come upon you." Through the working of the Spirit in the church the kingdom will be restored to Israel. This must be our concern for Israel, that they will repent and function in their calling to be a kingdom of priests, that for which God has chosen them.

ISRAEL'S CONVERSION IS IMPERATIVE

The apostles do not preach a two-way doctrine. It isn't: Jews will be justified by the keeping of the law, but Gentiles by faith in Christ.

Peter certainly did call Israel to repentance; Acts 2:38, 3:19. This repentance and turning back is the condition for the times of refreshing, for the time of peace. He in no uncertain terms tells the Jewish people that salvation is only possible by the Name of Jesus; Acts 4:12.

The author of the letter to the Hebrews explains the fulfilment of the old covenant by the new covenant to those who have knowledge of God's speaking to the fathers by the prophets, Hebr. 1:1, i.e. to the children of Israel.

Paul time and again assures us, and also the Jews, that justification is not by the works of the law, but through faith in Christ Jesus; Gal. 2:15, 16. The gospel is the power of God for salvation to everyone who believes, to the Jew first and also to the Greek; Rom. 1:16. All who base their faith on Him will not be ashamed, for there is no distinction between Jew and Greek; Rom. 10:11, 12. Israel needs salvation and cleansing of all her backslidings, idolatry and ungodliness, of her iniquities, transgressions, uncleannesses and stubbornness, as the prophets said; Ez. 36:29; Ez. 37:23; Isa. 59:20.

When Israel comes to faith in Jesus her Messiah, she will be grafted in again into her own cultivated olive tree; Rom. 11:23, 24.

So, Israel must receive Jesus in faith. This is what her conversion means. This is her acceptance and will be her fullness.

FROM FULLNESS TO FULLNESS

The Gentile Christian church must come into the fullness of God and so all Israel will come into *her* fullness and destiny; Rom. 11:12, 26. When Israel accepts Jesus as her Messiah, God will fill her with His grace, power, wisdom and Spirit, Ez. 36:27, with gifts and the latter rain, Hos. 6:3, salvation from her sins, Mt. 1:21, and deliverance from her enemies; Zech. 14:3; Ez. 28:25, 26. He will intervene in Israel's situation with powerful acts for the sake of His Name, before all the nations, "It is not for your sake, O house of Israel, that I am about to act, but for the sake of my holy name, (…) And I will vindicate the holiness of my great name, (…) And the nations will know that I am the Lord, declares the Lord God, when through you I vindicate my holiness before their eyes." Ez. 36:22, 23. And so all nations will learn to know Him, will seek Him and ask of Him. Israel's fullness is God's fulfilling action with Israel upon their faith in Jesus. It will be greater riches for the world; Rom. 11:12, 15. Through the restoration of the fallen hut of David the rest of mankind will seek the Lord; Acts 15:17. When Israel acknowledges Jesus as her King, the whole territory of David's kingdom will come under the rule and sway of Jesus. Then all nations will let themselves be taught from Jerusalem in the ways of the Lord; Isa. 2:2, 3. "Many peoples and strong nations shall come to seek the Lord of hosts in Jerusalem and to entreat the favor of the Lord." Zech. 8:22.

Israel's conversion will usher in the kingdom of peace. "Then the remnant of Jacob shall be in the midst of many peoples like dew from the Lord, like showers on the grass." Mic. 5:7.

Israel will be a blessing to the nations because God will give her His salvation; Zech. 8:13. Israel's fullness and destiny, her becoming a blessing for the world will be God's answer to her declaration: "Blessed is He who comes in the Name of the Lord." Mt. 23:39. They will see Jesus' delivering action and experience how He will make them to be a blessing.

Peter says to Israel: "Repent therefore, and turn back, that your sins may be blotted out, that times of refreshing may come from the presence of the Lord, and that he may send the Christ appointed for you, Jesus,…" Acts 3:19, 20. Here Peter clearly sets forth the sequence: first repentance and turning back, then times of refreshing, and finally the coming of Jesus. We must empty ourselves and completely surrender to Jesus, so that He may fill us with His fullness, so that through our fullness Israel also may come to fullness.

HALLOWED BE YOUR NAME

If peace on earth, Jesus' blessing by way of Israel, depends on Israel's repentance and turning, shouldn't our prayer and aim be for the salvation of Israel?

We too are a kingdom of priests, 1 Pet. 2:9, a nation of mediators in the service of God. In the first place our mediation, our priesthood must be directed by God's Name, by God's fulfilling deeds for the sake of Israel. In the first place Jesus teaches us to pray for the sanctification of God's Name. So, our aim and desire must be directed at the fulfilment of God's promises made to the patriarchs and for the restoration of the kingdom of priests to Israel; Acts 1:6-11; Isa. 61:6; Ex. 19:5, 6, for the whole earth belongs to God.

Therefore, in the first place our priesthood should be directed at the restoration of *their* priesthood.

ONE IN THE LAMB OF GOD

At the Lord's Supper, pleading the power of the blood of atonement, we must pray for fullness so that Israel may be saved, and pray for forgiveness of Jacob's ungodliness, Rom. 11:26, 27. We must also pray for the sanctification of God's Name, creating the conditions for the restoration of Israel's calling to be a kingdom of priests, so that they will be able to proclaim the Lamb of God to the world.

As Gentile Christians we must unite. Jesus wants our unity in Him and in the Father. That is what He prayed for. He expects that in our unity His being sent by the Father will be revealed; John 17:21, 23.

All those who have been reconciled by the blood of the Lamb *are* one. We can seal and show forth this unity by passing on to each other the cup of thanksgiving and by not allowing ourselves to be kept divided by all kinds of ecclesiastical rules and regulations, which are standing in the way of the fulfilment of Christ's prayer.

Tea is not poured into a cracked cup. Neither does God pour out His fullness into a torn and divided Christianity. Only into a church that unitedly pleads the power of the blood of atonement, and humbly confesses its guilt, God is able to pour out His fullness, the power of the Holy Spirit, so that the messiahship of Jesus and His mission is being revealed to Israel. Then we also may pass the cup to them. There is for Israel also reconciliation in the blood of the Lamb.

Gentiles and Jews together will become one. One flock under one Shepherd, one dwelling place for God by the Spirit, one Temple without a dividing wall, Eph. 2:14, one olive tree; Romans 11.

From Rev. 11:1 it becomes apparent that this temple once again is restored and is measurable. Her restoration paves the way for the kingdom of peace. Her restoration by the blood of Jesus binds Satan.

In the apostasy after the millennium the temple, the church of Jew and Gentile, as far as she has stayed faithful to her Lord, will be persecuted in Satan's last offensive. She is measured, or in other words, registered and kept by God from the evil one, so that she will not be tempted and deceived.

However, the outer court is excluded. Christians who do not know the intimate fellowship with God, whose trust in God has waned, will be misled; the outer court will be trodden. The two witnesses from chapter 11 are *(to me)* representatives of Jew and Gentile. They are a kind of Moses and Elijah-figure. They illustrate faithfulness and martyrdom in the short half-time, the resurrection as well as the rapture of the church. The faithful Jew and Gentile together will experience the rapture. There are no phases in the rapture. Not first a rapture of the Gentile Christian church before the millennium, and then after the millennium a rapture of the Messiah-believing Jews. Together we are *one* temple, kept from temptation and in the end are taken home together.

FALL, RISING AND SPOKEN AGAINST

Simeon prophesied concerning the three great turnings in history. "Behold, this Child is destined for the fall and rising of many in Israel, and for a sign which will be spoken against," Lk. 2:34 [NKJV].

The crucifixion of Jesus was the *fall* of Israel. This fall caused salvation to come to the Gentiles; Rom. 11:11.

When Israel repents and accepts Jesus, then this will be her *rising*. Ezek. 37:1-14 speaks about that rising. Hosea 6:1-2 also is about Israel's rising: "Come, let us return to the Lord; for he has torn us, that he may heal us; he has struck us down, and he will bind us up. After two days he will revive us; on the third day he will *raise* us up, that we may live before him."

After the times of refreshing, this great *sign* confirming the validity of His death on the cross throughout the ages that Jesus will have raised in the fullness of the Gentiles and the restoration of Israel, once again will be *spoken against* by the Antichrist. His distorted gospel will be in contradiction to the biblical gospel. However, the end will then come speedily. The denial will last but a short time. Until the coming of Jesus.

God's Name in the Apocalypse[1]

He who is and who was and who is to come

The Apocalypse is a revelation of God's Name, of His faithfulness to His covenant with Israel. It is not by chance that the Name I AM WHO I AM is put to this book as God's signature. Rev. 1:4 "Grace to you and peace from him WHO IS AND WHO WAS AND WHO IS TO COME." Rev. 1:8 " 'I am the Alpha and the Omega,' says the Lord God, 'WHO IS AND WHO WAS AND WHO IS TO COME, the Almighty.' "

When the end result of the whole of God's program has come, then all of creation sings: "Holy, holy, holy, is the Lord God Almighty, WHO WAS AND IS AND IS TO COME!" Rev. 4:8.

His faithful, active presence encompasses all ages.

God's Name forever stands for: exodus through the blood of the Passover Lamb, deliverance and salvation by Jesus. The other side of the coin is God's judgment upon all those who reject the Passover Lamb. Our salvation is through the Name of Jesus, the redeeming Passover Lamb.

This Name will be spoken against by the Antichrist. The Lord shows in how He named the beast from the sea who "was, and is not, and is about to rise," Rev. 17:8, that this beast's program is but a sly imitation of God's Name and program.

Whoever calls upon the Name of the Lord will be saved; Joel 2:32. Not only those who just mention this Name or only confess it with their mouth, but all those who truly trust upon the content and meaning of that Name.

Exodus in the Apocalypse

That the Apocalypse reveals God's Name can also be seen in the exodus events announced in it. In Lev. 26:18 and in Deut. 28:60 YHWH threatens Israel with a sevenfold punishment as well as with Egyptian plagues if they forget His covenant. God does not forget His covenant. When Israel rejects the Lamb of God, it receives a reverse exodus. Exile is the result. They are struck by a sevenfold action of the trumpeting angels, whose plagues clearly remind us of the Egyptian plagues; Rev. 8 and 9. However, the plagues are not meant to destroy Israel, but to call Israel to repentance and

---

[1] What I write in this chapter can be found in more detail and with much greater clarity in the prophetic book *"The seven Shofarim in the Apocalypse"* by A.A. Leenhouts, 2010. ISBN 978-90-7301-15-2. This book is available at Testimony and Unity Foundation (Stichting Getuigenis en Eenheid), www.getuigeniseneenheid.nl/books.html.

return. God's punishments are signs; Deut. 28:46. The plagues carry a message. These signs will have to tell Israel that they have become unfaithful to God by rejecting the Passover Lamb. So, the reverse exodus is meant to bring about a new exodus, a bringing back to God. However, the six plagues of Rev. 8 and 9, just as the nine plagues over Egypt, do not have any effect; Rev. 9:20.

INTERMEZZO EVENT

But before the seventh angel sounds the trumpet and the last judgments are released, YHWH will give through Christ Jesus a totally different action, an intermezzo event, a restoration event announced by another mighty angel; Rev. 10. The angel's feet lay claim to the whole world. He lays claim to Israel as well as the nations as God's property. His prophetic call is international. He is clothed with heavenly authority, wrapped in a cloud. The rainbow, reminding us of God's faithfulness to His covenant with Israel and the world, is over his head. And his face is lit up like the sun. With this the Lord shows that His face will lovingly light up over the world, that in world history a new day will dawn, a day of peace. And as with Israel's exodus from Egypt the last plague had the power to deliver and overcome, and the blood of the lamb had the power to protect, so also this other intermezzo event of the angel will deliver Israel as well as the nations from this Satanic power grab through the power of the blood of the Passover Lamb. With this God will confirm His Name I AM WHO I AM.

AFIKOMEN — HIDDEN PASSOVER BREAD

Originally in Israel it was the custom that in the Passover celebration the father would hide a piece of the Passover bread. After the Seder meal this piece had to be searched for and found. Likewise, the heavenly Father also has hidden something in Revelation 10. Passover bread! John was not allowed to write down what the seven thunders spoke. He had to seal this up, hide it as it were. But this mystery will be revealed before the restoration of Israel. It will lead to the restoration of Israel as well as to the rebuilding of God's temple. Israel will find the hidden piece of Passover bread. Jesus will be identified as the Passover Lamb!

Israel will discover whom they have pierced, the One whose bones were not broken. The great family Father took care that the bones of Jesus remained unbroken, as was prescribed for all Passover lambs. Israel will come to recognise the divine Passover Lamb by way of the fullness of the Gentiles, by way of God's merciful intervention in the Gentile Christian church, in their becoming one and by their united confession of Jesus' sacrifice.

The thunders are an indication of His royal glory, and of the binding of Satan. Compare this with John 12:28-31.

Jesus ascended into heaven in order to bring all things to fullness, to fulfil all things. This too He will fulfil before He returns.

ELIJAH

When we consider the return of Jesus in connection with God's Name, then we also must think of Elijah. Elijah's name means: My God is Yahweh. By his actions it became clear to Israel that Yahweh was the only God.

Malachi concludes his prophecies with the announcement of the coming of Elijah, for God does not want to strike the land with a curse, but instead desires to bring the people back by way of Elijah's prophetic actions; Mal. 4:5, 6.

According to Jewish tradition Elijah will be a forerunner before the redemption of the whole world. John the Baptist was such a forerunner, such a preparer of the way before the coming of King Jesus. However, Jesus proclaimed that once more another Elijah will come; Mt. 17:12. The appearance of the herald angel in Revelation 10 implies an elianic action. His action will result in restoration, Israel's regrafting and restoration and the restoration of the nations. The whole world, earth and sea, will become the domain of King Jesus! The darkness must yield, for in Rev. 10 the sun is shining. For all those who fear God's Name, the Sun of Righteousness shall arise; Mal. 4:2. Through this elianic action Israel will be brought back to God's covenant, by the power of the blood of the new covenant. Through this action Israel will call out: Jesus is Lord! Israel will become a partaker of the hidden Passover Bread, the mystery of Rev. 10.

NO MORE DELAY

Next the angel swears that, once it is fulfilled what God proclaimed by His prophets concerning the breakthrough of the Kingdom of peace upon Israel's conversion, there will be no more delay. Then there is nothing that will stop the Lord from coming back. When all of humanity has learned to know Him, and then once again turns away from God, then there is an end to God's long-suffering. Then at the last trump, the seventh trumpet, the Lord returns. Then the Lord will provide for the last exodus, the plagues with the seven bowls of God's wrath, Rev. 15 and 16, judgments upon all the antichristian powers, announced by God's two elianic witnesses. To the church this will mean that during this time of tribulation the rapture will occur, the exodus to the heavenly home of the Father, again also by the power of the blood of the Lamb. With this God's Name is sanctified once again.

COME, LORD JESUS

Jesus says, "Surely I am coming soon." Counting from eternity His coming is soon. During the time of great tribulation, in times of direst need, the Lord, upon their distressful cry: "Come, Lord Jesus!" will certainly not delay long. And John agrees with this when he ends with: "Amen. Come, Lord Jesus!" This is the conclusion of the Bible, the conclusion of God's war-annals, the conclusion of the battle, the end of our age. To us this is still far removed. Right at the very end of the Book and of history.

When I pray: "Amen, come, Lord Jesus," then I am looking for a coming that is closer by. He will come in the Spirit to make the church one. He comes in the Spirit to fill a humbled church with the fullness of God, to reveal His messiahship to Israel. He will come in the Spirit to turn Israel back to Himself and to restore her to her royal priesthood, so that they will proclaim the Lamb of God among all nations. He comes in the Spirit to bind Satan by the united confession of the Lord's death and resurrection, and to bring peace on earth.

This coming as in days past will be such a great intervention of God that Jesus will be glorified! His preponderance will be evident. His opponents will be ruled against! He will be identified as the Lamb and the Lion of Judah! God's Name will be sanctified!

This intervention of God will be a manifestation and confirmation of the validity and legal authority of Jesus' offer of atonement for all ages.

PRELUDE

The Lord also has set a day for this intervention, which He Himself has determined.

Before the end comes, the Name, I AM WHO I AM SAVES, will once more be seen to be true and will act as a powerful worldwide missionary appeal. Once more the Lord will show that salvation is only to be found in His Name!

The apostasy and lawlessness of our time is but a foreshadow of the apostasy and lawlessness of the last days. And the persecution of Christians happening here and there and the judgments and catastrophes … "all these are but the beginning of the birth pains," Mt. 24:8, they are but a prelude of the great tribulation and the final judgment on the last day. Although we may discern beastlike antichristian traits in the World Council of Churches and in the United Nations, and although the WCC does act like the prophet to the United Nations, which she presents to the world as the answer to all our needs and as the salvation and only hope for the future, they are but prefigurations of the political and religious powers of the last days, who are portrayed as beastlike figures risen from the sea and the earth.

The battle of Gog and Magog from Ezekiel 38 and 39, along with the many nations who will advance against Israel, is also for the sake of God's holy Name so that YHWH will be made known in all the earth. They will be defeated by God and this is but a shadow of the war which Satan will enter into with the saints in the last days; Rev. 20:8, 9. The binding of Satan, Rev. 20:2, 3, is a foretaste of his final judgment in the lake of fire; Rev. 20:10.

The breakthrough of the Millennial Kingdom of Peace, the Sabbath for the nations, the times of refreshing, is a blueprint and guarantee for the eternal kingdom. This eternal kingdom will start at the return of Jesus with power and glory.

The new heaven and new earth mentioned in Isa. 65:17-25, wherein yet sinners live, wherein man is born and yet dies, is but a pledge for the new heaven and the new earth of Rev. 21.

The whole state of affairs of our days does very much look like the time of the end, but yet is not the end itself. It is only the announcement and proof, the cast-forward glow of the terrible events of just before the return of Christ. It is the longing for the sanctification of God's Name and the glorification of Jesus that makes me pray: Maranatha, come, Lord Jesus!

PRAISE HIS NAME!

The church must be focused on the unity of the body, and must consider her calling and function, so that we will be a people for God's Name, so that God's Name will be hallowed, so that Israel will acknowledge that Jesus comes in the Name of the Lord.

"In the path of your judgments, O Lord, we wait for you; your name and remembrance are the desire of our soul," Isa. 26:8. "From the rising of the sun to its setting, the name of the Lord is to be praised!" Hallelujah! "Praise, O servants of the Lord, praise the name of the Lord! Blessed be the name of the Lord from this time forth and forevermore!" Ps. 113:3, 1, 2.

Tested against the Bible

A commission

Today there are many visions in circulation about the last days. Future expectations originating from and based on a vision or dream, which, with the use of proof texts, appear to be biblically based. Or visions coming forth from someone's own thoughts and conclusions, often are considered as coming from the Holy Spirit. And visions received because the Lord today does speak prophetically.

To the average Christian it is terribly difficult to find a truly biblical perspective for the future from all these many different expectations. Yet the Lord tells us to: "test everything; hold fast what is good." 1 Thess. 5:21. And: "test the spirits to see whether they are from God," 1 John 4:1. For if they have originated from our own inner being, or maybe from a deceiving spirit, then we must reject this vision for the future. But if it truly comes from God, then we must pay attention to it. In any case we must keep that what is good.

As a layperson we should not wait if our church leaders, our pastors and elders will or will not accept the proffered vision. Of course, they carry the greatest responsibility to listen, to examine and to judge — they do watch over our souls — but they are very busy! They will not always have time to do this. As laypersons we should not hide behind this. The commission to test everything is also given to us.

Not so simple

Testing ascertains if the vision is biblical or not. Not just when scriptural passages are used, for that in itself does not say very much. The devil too quotes the Bible.

Scriptures should not be taken out of context. The exegesis of these Scriptures should line up with the totality of the biblical witness. The exegesis should be in line with how Jesus understood Scripture. What is meant literal should be literally understood. But what is meant metaphorically, should not be taken in a literal way. The prophets, as did Jesus, used many parables and symbolic language. And especially the Apocalypse is filled with symbols and depictions from God. However, these metaphors or depictions are often found elsewhere in Scripture.

THE NECESSITY OF THE HOLY SPIRIT

In order to know if something is from God or from another source, much prayer is needed. With testing we are totally dependent on the Holy Spirit, Who will teach us all things and guide us into all truth, if we are willing to hear. The Lord Himself will have to make clear what He means. Therefore, always do test with much prayer.

Also pay attention when you test if Jesus is recognizable in the vision. Does He reign? Is He the One who has all power? Does His intercessory function come to justice in the vision? And is He honoured above all? For the Holy Spirit desires to glorify Jesus! And He glorifies Him from out of His suffering and death. We know that Satan fears the Gospel of the cross, for that is and will be his downfall. When Jesus' work of atonement is ignored or belittled, or even is spoken against, then in any case the vision is not from the Lord.

DIFFERENT FUTURE EXPECTATIONS

We must out of hand reject a certain number of views as being unbiblical.

NO REPLACEMENT

For example, 'replacement theology'.

Of course, in faith we may see ourselves as spiritual Israel; Rom. 4:11b, 12, 16-18, *provided* we do not forget natural Israel. We may not place ourselves *in the place* of Israel and so push them out of the unconditional covenant, as if God no longer looks after His people. That amounts to the profaning of His Name! The ancient prophets certainly did prophesy concerning natural Israel. So, in the first-place, every promise mentioned by them counts for the Jewish people. For example, Jer. 31:31-34 and Ezek. 36:25-28, Scriptures which we gladly apply to ourselves, in the first place do concern the house of Israel, the Jewish people. It is said of the Lamb that "he shall see his offspring; he shall prolong his days; the will of the Lord shall prosper in his hand." Isa. 53:10. So, Jesus, the Lamb of God, will fulfil every promise made to Israel. Jesus did not lose sight of them, but in His love, faithfulness and mercy, He will have His way with them (also in judgment) to bring them to their ultimate salvation and restoration. He also did give His life for them! Israel too will live by His grace and mercy and will yet have a wonderful future and be ready to serve and be a blessing to the nations; see for example Isa. 2:2, 3; 27:6; 55:5; Jer. 33:9 to name some Scriptures from among the many.

Israel is called God's holy people. This is not because of how good they are. But they have been called to holiness based on God's sovereign choice. God Himself does give Israel this peculiar position.

God Himself also chose the land of Canaan to be their land; a land in which He will reveal Himself as the Holy One.

In God's saving deeds the holy people and the holy land belong together.

What does it mean for Israel to be a holy nation, a nation set aside? As the eldest, the firstborn, in a family is counted as the representative for all, so Israel, as firstborn — Ex. 4:22, 23 — is counted as representative for the nations of the world. Israel must be God's witness to the nations. The nations will learn to know God through Israel. The nations will be able to see who God is by what He does with Israel. Israel must be a blessing for the nations because God blesses them. God, by way of Israel, wants to bless the world. Israel has a serving, intercessory and priestly calling; Ex, 19:5, 6.

Israel will be blessed when she walks in God's ways but cursed if she leaves His ways. To be blessed holds in that God is with her. To be cursed means that God has let her go and has given her up to the powers of darkness. God deals with Israel in blessing as well as in cursing; in when Israel cleaves to Him, as well as when she forgets Him and choses her own way. However, Israel will never be able to get away from her election. This covenant is unconditional.

We can tell from what happens to Israel in how her relationship is with God. Is the relationship between God and Israel good, then she will be able to rejoice in peace, liberty and safety, in good harvests and blessings in the promised land; Dt. 28:1-14. However, is the relationship between Israel and God bad or broken, then the holy land will be at enmity with her; poor harvests, no security and the land will even vomit her out; Dt. 28:15-68; Lev. 20:22.

As long as Israel knows this hidden relationship with God, election can be experienced as a privilege. But outside of God, this being chosen as a holy nation will be like a heavy burden and a terror. For as the firstborn, the representative nation, they will receive double chastisements and double blessings, Isa. 40:2; Isa. 61:7; Jer. 16:18; Rev. 8:6, as the oldest son in a family inherits a double portion; Dt. 21:17.

The *degree* to which Israel will be disciplined tells us something about the importance of her calling and election to be a holy nation before God. At all times we will have to respect that high position. The *degree* of her discipline also tells us something about the *seriousness* of her falling away from a holy God, how offensive this is in God's eye. To us this is an example and a warning; 1 Cor. 10:6 and 11. From this discipline we may know the fear of the Lord.

Israel is even so representative that as long as this nation exists, creation too will remain. If this holy nation would disappear from the earth, then the world would also cease to exist. Israel will be as long as the world remains. "Thus says the Lord, who gives the sun for light by day and the fixed order of the moon and the stars for light by night, who stirs up the sea so that its waves roar the Lord of hosts is his name: 'If this fixed order departs from before me,' declares the Lord, 'then shall the offspring of Israel cease from being a nation before me forever.' " Jer. 31:35, 36.

Whoever violates Israel, interferes with God's people and actually assaults God Himself! "…he who touches you touches the apple of His eye." Zech. 2:8b.

He who blesses Israel, will be blessed. And whosoever curses Israel, will be cursed; Gen. 12:3.

These principles do have the force of law from the Holy One until the very last day. The attitude of the nations towards Israel is decisive for the continuing existence, security and peace of the world. Every power that desires to eradicate Israel is a danger to all humanity. And especially to itself.

Also, Israel's attitude towards God has powerful effects on the world. For example, when Israel, because of God's great wrath, is thrown "like a great mountain, burning with fire" into the sea of nations, really into exile, then this effects many peoples; Rev. 8:8, 9.

Throughout the ages, since her rejection of God's Servant, Israel has had to suffer greatly. Their being chosen has become to them a living hell. This too has not left the nations untouched.

Satan does have knowledge of God's plans but only in a limited way. He knows that Israel is chosen for a holy purpose. Would all the churches know this as well! He knows that the time is approaching (but when exactly??), that Israel will be restored and will be used by the Lord for the breakthrough of His Kingdom. This is not what Satan wants. By his attempts in exterminating the Jewish people, he tries to make the Kingdom of God an impossibility on earth. Because Israel was given up by the Lord, Satan was able to strike them terrifyingly hard!

How Israel's Messiah must have suffered in seeing His people being destroyed! How He must have been bursting to save them! But He had to keep Himself to the sovereign program of the Father. However, after a third of the chosen people had perished, He could call a halt to the destroyer. Two-thirds of Israel escaped, were saved from this hell by the merciful grace of the Lord, although they refused to know Him. That two-thirds of the people were saved tells me that God *lives*! He *is* faithful to His covenant.

I am glad that the Lord did not wait to intervene until half the people were destroyed, for that would have meant that Satan is as strong as the Lord. Now that two-thirds of God's people were saved, it is clear that the Lord is at least twice as powerful as Satan. And I am glad that the Lord does not wait for acknowledgement before He sparingly intervenes.

Besides Rev. 8 the Bible speaks in many places about 'a third', for example Ezek. 5:2, 12. A third always means that there is a limit to God's punishment. God's judgments have a merciful limitation. For His own sake the Lord will never allow Israel to be totally eradicated; Isa. 48:9-11; Ezek. 20:8, 9, 14, 21, 22, 43, 44.

As long as Israel disregards her sacred position, and rather functions as a secular State, instead of walking in God's holy Way — serving the nations and being a blessing —the world will remain in turmoil.

But when Israel does return to her God, she will be a blessing as a holy nation in the midst of the nations; Isa. 62:12. "And as you have been a byword of cursing among the nations, O house of Judah and house of Israel, so will I save you, and you shall be a blessing. Fear not, but let your hands be strong." Zech. 8:13.

Then they will receive a *double portion*, Isa. 61:7, and will be doubly restored, Zech. 9:12, as a sign of her high status. Then Jerusalem, the holy city, will become an international, religious centre, Zech. 8:20-23; Isa. 2:2-5, for then the Lord will be *with* Israel.

To cling to Replacement theology is arrogance and shows a lack of understanding of God's love, faithfulness and mercy. This doctrine has caused great grief and suffering for Israel. Because of this arrogance we ourselves have become the cause that Israel, after two thousand years, still has no understanding concerning her Messiah.

Whoever clings to replacement theology better pays attention to Paul's warning in Rom. 11:17-22 "…do not be arrogant toward the branches, (…) it is not you who support the root, but the root that supports you. (…) So, do not become proud, but fear." Of what should we be afraid? That He will not spare us either! That He also will cut us off! We must remain in the mercy that we have received, the same mercy that is available for Israel.

How can we count on God's faithfulness if we deny His faithfulness to Israel?! Rom. 3:3; Isa. 46:3, 4; Isa. 9:16; Jer. 31:35-37. God is faithful to His people! Replacement theology maligns God's Name and the love of Christ.

ONLY ONE WAY FOR SALVATION

The heretical Two-Way doctrine is clearly in contradiction with the New Testament. It is not true that Israel will be saved by keeping the law of Moses. Israel always had to live by faith. Living from faith and through grace is valid for the Jew as well as for the Gentile; Isa. 30:15; Rom. 1:16, 17; Rom. 10:11-13; 1 Cor. 1:23, 24; Gal. 3:36-28; Eph. 2:18; Col. 3:11. Christ, the Lamb of God, did not only come for Gentile Christians, but for many centuries before already had been promised to Israel; Isa. 53.

They too need the Saviour and atonement through His blood, Mt. 1:21; cp. Zech. 13:1. Jesus also died for them and will heal them.

Without Jesus Israel has lost the way; John 8:19, 47; John 3:36; John 14:6.

The Two-Way or Dual Covenant teaching devalues Christ's offer on the cross.

NOT LEFT TO OUR OWN DEVICES

The thought that God would have withdrawn Himself from this world and has left everything to our own responsibility, as if we ourselves are able to bring about the dreams of the prophets, is a denial of and insult to God. This teaching denigrates the power, faithfulness and love of our Lord. This doctrine desecrates the Name of God. Specifically, in His deeds and actions God makes Himself a Name. Isn't this the uniqueness of YHWH that He concerns Himself with people! His Name guarantees the fulfilment of all His promises! Ezek. 20:44; Isa. 29:23; 60:22b. What He says He will do! Isa. 46:10, 11b "I have spoken, and I will bring it to pass; I have purposed, and I will do it." He watches over His word to perform it; Jer. 1:12.

God is a jealous God, Who will not give His glory to another; Isa. 42:8. What we want to bring about by our own wisdom, power and pride will not stand. The Lord will take this honour away from us. He Himself will confirm His word, Isa. 44:24, 25, 26a.

It is man's pride to think that we are able to bring about peace on earth, possibly by having peace conferences or treaties of cooperation and or with a one-world government. It is Jesus who makes every promise true; 2 Cor. 1:20. It is Jesus who will give to Israel the promised land in peace. Because of our lack of self-knowledge, we do overestimate ourselves; Psa. 14:1-3.

Also, we certainly do underestimate God's adversary! As long as Satan is not bound, peace on earth will be a fleeting thing. He will be overcome by the power of Christ's blood shed on Golgotha; 1 John 3:8; Rev. 12:11.

When Israel accepts the Lamb of God, there will be a turning in the lives and affairs of the nations; Rom. 11:15. Without God there is no fulfilment.

Without the Son of David, the Prince of Peace, there will be no peace on earth.

THE RETURN

When reading the prophets, it is noticeable that God's promises bringing 'a change in the fate of Israel', the return and living in peace almost always go together. How often are return and salvation not mentioned in the same breath! Jer. 30:10b "Jacob shall return and have quiet and ease, and none shall make him afraid." Jer. 46:27; 31:1-14; 32:37-41; 23:3-6; Isa. 35:10; 51:11; Ezek. 39:25-29.

Israel did return to the land of promise. What Christian did not rejoice over that? We certainly wished for Israel to have a place of rest!

But, peace has been far from present!

The State of Israel is continually under threat. And sometimes the situation in the Middle East also threatens the whole world. Israel is called to be a blessing, but it often is a threat to peace. Has God's word become null and void? Why did the Lord bring Israel back, but did not give her peace? This question created in me great turmoil. I continually prayed to the Lord about this: 'You have given them the promised land. Why don't You give them peace now as well? Isn't this what You promised?' The Lord made me read the story of Jacob. He had been promised the firstborn blessing, but he took this in a deceptive way. Consequently, his life was threatened. The land too is promised to Israel! But they live in the land under a continual threat. Suddenly the Lord showed me clearly: they *took* the land! They did not *receive* the land. That is why there is no peace! They themselves have wanted to make God's promises true, without trustingly waiting for God's leading and fulfilling actions. Israel's not living in peace does not say anything about God's untrustworthiness but says everything about Israel's obstinacy.

But then where can we see any of God's deeds? He has helped Israel to win every war against her. But peace has eluded her grasp. The Lord, because of His Name, prevents them of being driven into the sea. However, security has failed to materialize.

When Israel was about to celebrate her twenty-year anniversary, I heard that they were planning to parade all captured war materiel from the June 1967 war through the streets of Jerusalem. 'Lord, it was You who helped Israel to win this war! What Israel is planning to do is idolatry! Please, send a prophet to Israel to warn her!' I was very upset about this. I was worried. Then the Lord audibly told me: 'Let Israel go ahead and worship her idols.' I had trouble in receiving that word. I said indignantly: 'Don't You care about Israel anymore?' And, as I often do when I am confused, I grabbed for a Bible and it opened to Ezekiel 20. My eye fell on verse 39:

"As for you, O house of Israel," thus says the Lord God, "Go, serve everyone his idols; but later you will surely listen to Me, and My holy name you will profane no longer." [NASB] I was certainly surprised with that. It was saying the same thing! It comforted me to read: "…but later you will surely listen to Me." So, a change will come. I knew the Lord will send a prophet, exactly as I had asked Him in my prayer.

Looking closer at this Scripture portion it appears that twice a gathering is mentioned. Ezek. 20:33-38 speaks of a gathering out from the countries with *wrath poured out*. And indeed, how has Israel been gathered! Because of an unimaginable horror they have sought refuge in the ancient land of promise. But there too the Lord enters into judgment with them; Ezek. 20:35.

Only when Israel listens to the voice of the Lord will there be a gathering *as a pleasing aroma;* Ezek. 20:39-42.

This is the expectation we may have.

However, Ezek. 20:32 yet applies: "What is in your mind shall never happen—the thought, 'Let us be like the nations…' " Israel is and remains God's chosen people. They are His peculiar people, His 'Am Segullah', and therefore never to be equated with the other nations. The secular State and secular Zionism will never give them peace. No matter what peace accords may have been made, as long as Israel does not listen to her God, her Saviour, the promised land will remain a thorn in her side.

"And the ransomed of the Lord shall return and come to Zion with singing; everlasting joy shall be upon their heads; they shall obtain gladness and joy, and sorrow and sighing shall flee away." Isa. 35:10. Their Saviour already has paid the price for Israel. The singing, the joy and the gladness are there for them, when they travel on God's highway, Isa. 35:8. We know who is that 'Way'. Jer. 23:3, 4 says: "Then I will gather the remnant of my flock out of all the countries where I have driven them, and I will bring them back to their fold, (…) and they shall fear no more, nor be dismayed." This too the Lord certainly will fulfil when Israel acknowledges the *righteous Branch* from Jer. 23:5 as her King.

We must consider secular Zionism as an unbiblical vision. It goes against the holiness of the Lord. It is a denial of the love of God, Who has given His Son for them. It is a profaning of God's Name.

Presently Israel's situation is at a halfway point, Ezek. 20:39 (NASB) "but later you will…" Let us pray that this time will speedily come! For then God's Name no longer will be profaned! And then Israel no longer will have to suffer.

By faith, not by sight

The expectation that *Israel will accept Jesus when they see Him at His coming* does relieve us from our responsibility for Israel. But we are called to be a people for God's Name! We are witnesses of the crucified and risen Lord! Israel must be able to recognize Jesus in and through us. The Spirit will show Jesus to them through His actions with us. Paul expects Israel's salvation upon God's fulfilling action with the Gentiles — the fullness of the Gentiles — Rom. 11:25. Furthermore, Jesus says that the power of the Holy Spirit is needed for the restoration of the kingdom to Israel; Acts 1:8. The Holy Spirit will convict Israel of sin, because they have rejected their Messiah. And of righteousness, because He now is with the Father; John 16:8-10.

Sometimes Zech. 13:6 is used to show that Jesus will convince Israel by showing His wounds. "And if one asks him, 'What are these wounds on your back?' he will say, 'The wounds I received in the house of my friends.'"

However, this Scripture is not about the Messiah at all, but concerns the false prophets, who were struck when it appeared that their messages were not true. When taken in context, Zech. 13:6 can never be applied to Jesus. This Scripture has been taken out of context, and alas, has taken on a life of itself.

Israel too must believe without seeing; John 6:40; Rom. 10:11-13 and 11:23. This particular teaching of the physical and visible return of the Lord causing Israel to believe does a disservice to the love and holiness of Jesus. Whoever thinks in this manner is of no use for God's Name.

Judgment by fire?

There is a teaching circulating that before the Millennium a third of humanity will perish by nuclear fire. This point of view is based on Rev. 8:7; 9:15, 18; Isa. 66:15, 16; Mal. 4:1. This would in particular concern the apostate Christian West.

In the first place Rev. 8 and 9 are about Israel. God through Moses told Israel that He would chastise them sevenfold if they would not listen to Him; Lev. 26:18, 21, 24, 28. He would discipline them with the plagues of Egypt; Dt. 28:60. The Egyptian plagues announced by the seven angels with trumpets in Rev. 8 and 9 declare and *show* that Israel is under God's curse; Dt. 28:46. At the same time these plagues are an invitation to turn back to the Lord. These chapters should not be used to announce a judgment by nuclear fire over the Christian West.

It is true that we as Christians have wandered far from the Lord and have become conceited, and therefore are ripe for a judgment. But it is also true that Jesus on the cross has taken upon Himself God's burning wrath and anger. And when we in faith plead the blood of the Lamb over us, there also will be a passing by of the angel of death.

The Lord will pour out His burning wrath over all those who are against Him. But even when He threatens with fiery terms, then this still does not have to stand for nuclear fire. Is a nuclear disaster able to ensure peace? Would not the remaining two-thirds of mankind have to suffer in the coming generations of the after effects of this disaster? Such things as miscarriages, disabled people, deformities with plant, animal and human being. Is this what is called peace? God does not need an atomic bomb if He wants to punish, even if we are able to destroy all of humanity with it. If He really wants to punish with fire, He certainly can do this with heavenly fire, as He has done many a time in the past; Lev. 10:1, 2; Num. 16:35; 2 Kings 1:10, 12, 14.

God's wrath may burn like fire, but that doesn't mean that God in His wrath specifically sends fire. This expression depicts the intensity of God's wrath, which can manifest itself in many ways.

For example, in Deut. 32:22 the Lord says: "For a fire is kindled by my anger, and it burns to the depths of Sheol," but then it appears that He does not use His fire as punishment, but instead uses calamities, earthquakes, famine, war, pestilence and wild animals; Dt. 32:22-25.

This judgment is directed at Israel, who had neglected and left the Rock that brought them forth, verse 18. Furthermore, one of God's *arrows*, one of His punishments is that He will provoke Israel to jealousy by what is not a people, verse 21. This all because of the *fire* of His wrath. And when the prophet Isaiah says that Israel is set on fire all around, then these fiery terms imply captivity, pillaging and military force, but no fire; Isa. 42:25. In the same vein Isa. 66:15 and 16 do have to do with judgment, but not necessarily with fire. And certainly not with nuclear fire!

When Paul speaks about the church being God's temple, with Jesus as foundation, he warns that the Day of the Lord will disclose if any of the doctrines, rules and traditions build on it will survive or not, all that is from God or from man; 1 Cor. 3:12-15. Here it concerns spiritual construction, this temple will be cleansed by the fire of the Spirit. This is the same as what Malachi speaks of. On the Day of the Lord He will clean this spiritual house and will remove all that what is not of Him, refining and purifying, in order that they will be restored to a holy priesthood; Mal. 3:1-5. All those who have built recklessly, conceitedly and in pride, outside of God, will be put in the wrong, will be 'like stubble', over against those who have remained near to the Lord. All who fear God's Name will tread down, or triumph over the exalted, fraudulent and lost religious leaders, who build wrongly and whose work will not stand; Mal. 4:1, 2.

1 Cor. 3:15, Mal. 3:2,3 and 4:1 say the same thing. Israel as well as the Gentile Christian community will be purified and restored by the fire of the Holy Spirit. This will be a 'temple cleansing', not a nuclear judgment.

Doesn't Jesus Himself speak about fire in a spiritual manner, when He says: "I came to cast fire on the earth, and would that it were already kindled!" Lk. 12:49.
The expectation from Rev. 8 and 9 and Isa. 66 and Mal. 4 that a third of mankind will be destroyed by atomic fire should be rejected, because the spiritual speaking of the Lord has not been considered.

The doctrine of judgment by fire maligns the love of Christ and the value of His sacrificial blood.
On the other hand, Rev. Leenhouts holds out the prospect of a 'Carmel judgment'.[2] With this I mean an intervention by God, confronting His opponents — the apostates, self-willed and haughty — in such a manner that the conclusion only can be: Jesus is Lord!

It is the fire of the Holy Spirit that will fill a community gathering around the blood of atonement and remembering the death of Jesus, with love, grace and power, glorifying the Lamb of God and through it all exposing every 'ism' and 'mountain' and every religion that is not of Him: Mal. 4:1, 2; Rom. 11:25.

When we reflect the glory of the Lord, 2 Cor. 3:18, and the Spirit truly convicts because of Jesus, John 16:8, 14, and Israel in the day of their distress calls on Him, Jer. 30:7, then Israel too will experience a passing over of the angel of death, will experience salvation and deliverance.

REUNION

There is a movement that is looking for the so-called *lost tribes of Israel*. These Christians think that we in Western Europe belong to those ten lost tribes.

Ezekiel did speak about the two 'sticks' which the Lord would join together as one. The two-tribe kingdom of Judah and the ten-tribe kingdom of Israel or Ephraim will become one nation; Ezek. 37:15-23.

The Lord will fulfil every prophecy! No doubt about it.

But has this prophecy not already been fulfilled? Or must we expect a future fulfilment? At the end of 2 Chron. 36:23, Cyrus, the king of Persia, says: "Whoever is among you of all his people, may the Lord his God be with him. Let him go up." In all his kingdom Cyrus urged Israelites from *every tribe* to return in order to rebuild the temple of the Lord.

---

[2] A.A. Leenhouts: *Competition of The Altars*, 1984. ISBN: 90-9000-676-1. This book is available at Testimony and Unity Foundation (Stichting Getuigenis en Eenheid), www.getuigeniseneenheid.nl/books.html.

It was at that time that the prophecy of Ezekiel was fulfilled. From every tribe the Israelites went up, maybe not en masse, but whosoever felt himself called. "One from a city and two from a family," as Jeremiah prophesied in chapter 3:14. These Israelites from every tribe became one people, and later were called Jews. So not every Jew is descended from the tribe of Judah. Whoever did not feel himself called, but instead chose to remain in Assyria or Babylon, were in the end assimilated, and remained dispersed and became unrecognisable. James also takes into account the twelve tribes in the Dispersion, by addressing a letter to them; James 1:1.

When we read Ezekiel 37 from verse 23 onward then it appears that his prophecy has not been totally fulfilled yet. Similarly, Jer. 3:17 is not yet fulfilled. So, we may expect a further fulfilment. But do we have to expect for Jer. 3:18 a repetition of this fulfilment in a greater measure? A yet turning up of the ten lost tribes?

Once I prayed to the Lord concerning another Scripture: 'Lord, who is Ephraim?' and before I could say 'Amen', a voice from on high answered me: 'Ephraim is the community called forth from the Gentile world by the greater than Joseph, Jesus Christ.'

I don't want Replacement Theology. I don't want to put the Gentile Christian church in the place of natural Ephraim. Far be it from me. But by this answer my attention was directed away from natural Ephraim. We don't have to start looking for them. This is not our calling. This is God's responsibility. If He yet wants to fulfil this prophecy, then He will do that in His time and in His way. And this certainly *before* Jesus returns. However, this answer from heaven directed my attention once again to God's desire to join into one the Gentile Christian community with Israel, the Jewish people. It is our responsibility to strive for fullness in such a way that Israel will come to salvation, and that we'll be one in Christ according to Eph. 2:14-22, a dwelling place for God in the Spirit and according to Rom. 11:23, 24 as one olive tree, or after John 10:16, as one flock under one Shepherd, our King Jesus, David's Son; Ezek. 37:24.

Even if the further fulfilment still rests in God's hands, let us not be distracted by this from the Lord's priorities: 'to provoke them to jealousy', Rom. 11:11b. The unity of the church and subsequently the unity of Jew and Gentile is for today of more importance then the eventual coming together of the lost tribes.

TESTING OF THE ESCAPE THEORY

THE IMPLICATIONS OF THIS THEORY

The complicated *escape theology* is a chapter by itself, combined with the two-covenant doctrine. This teaching presupposes,

- that the great Tribulation will take place before the millennial kingdom of peace, because the period of the beast falls before the new heaven and the new earth of Rev. 21;

- that the Church will be raptured before the great Tribulation (because we will be kept from the hour of trial, Rev. 3:10), at the time of Jesus' hidden and first coming; this is the first phase of the return of the Lord (for He is coming as 'a thief in the night');

- that the Church then in heaven will celebrate the great wedding feast of the Lamb, while on earth the great tribulation rages (for at that time the one who restrains, the Holy Spirit, will no longer be there, and the lawless one will reveal himself, 2 Thess. 2:6-8);

- that then the one hundred forty-four thousand Jews will repent and turn (for Israel will turn back to God when the fullness of the Gentiles comes in, Rom. 11:25), whether during the great tribulation, or at the coming of Jesus (two variations);

- that Jesus will return physically after the great tribulation; this then is the second phase of His return ('with power and great glory', Mt. 24:30). He will come together with the saints, who will reign with Him as kings (Rev. 20:4);

- that the lawless one will perish at the second coming (2 Thess. 2:8);

- that the converted Jews will reign as kings either together with the saints, or that the saints may serve as stewards (there are again two variations) during the Millennium.

Much of this doctrine is debatable and we must categorically reject it as unbiblical, even when many biblical texts are used.

THE GREAT TRIBULATION AFTER THE MILLENNIUM, BEFORE THE ETERNAL KINGDOM

We clearly must distinguish between the eternal kingdom and the millennial kingdom of peace. The new heaven and the new earth of Revelation 21 is definitely not the same as the new heaven and the new earth of Isaiah 65, although some seem to think so. Rev. 21 speaks about the eternal kingdom where there are no sinners neither will there be death, see verses 4 and 8. Isaiah 65 deals with the kingdom of peace in our earthly time and does know of sinners and death, see verse 20.

The great tribulation occurs during the time of Satan's loosening, Rev. 20:7, after the Millennium; this is the period of the beast, Rev. 13-19, or the time of great trouble, Dan. 12:1, before the eternal kingdom.

Jesus says: "Immediately after the tribulation of those days the sun will be darkened, and the moon will not give its light, and the stars will fall from heaven, and the powers of the heavens will be shaken. Then will appear in heaven the sign of the Son of Man, …" etc. Mt. 24:29, 30. The shaking of the powers of heaven is the end of the world: Heb. 12:26, 27; see also 2 Pet. 3:10.

After the shattering of the power of the holy people the end will come; Dan. 12:7b. Therefore, the great tribulation takes place before the *end* of our world history. It is Satan's last attack on God's children, the seed of the woman.

NO RAPTURE BEFORE THE GREAT TRIBULATION

Forever Satan has it in for God's people, for the saints, the seed of the woman. Also in his last attack his aim is to destroy the church of Jew and Gentile, the saints; Rev. 12:17; 13:7; 18:24. Whoever does not worship the image of the Beast and has not received the mark of the beast, will be killed, Rev. 13:15b, or will be driven from society, 13:17. The Antichrist is even depicted as drunk "with the blood of the saints," the martyrs of Jesus"; Rev. 17:6.

So, the church is not saved from tribulation; 2 Tim. 3:12. Jesus even predicted this for us: "In the world you will have tribulation. But take heart; I have overcome the world." John 16:33. And: "If they persecuted me, they will also persecute you." John 15:20b; Lk. 21:12; Mt. 24:9, 21. In the next verse, Mt. 24:22, Jesus says that those days of the great tribulation will be cut short *for the sake* of the elect. Satan only has been granted a short time, Rev. 20:3b. The coming of Jesus will cut off Satan's work of destruction; Jesus, the Lamb of God, will come right in the middle of the tribulation to defeat all Satan's hordes; 2 Thess. 2:8; Rev. 17:14; 19:19-21; 20:10.

After the great tribulation, when Jesus comes, the angels will gather the elect, Mt. 24:31, to be taken, Mt. 24:40, 41. The elect Jesus will take to Himself at His coming, to be with Him forever, John 14:3. So the rapture is after the great tribulation.

TO BE KEPT IS NOT THE SAME AS BEING RAPTURED

Jesus does not pray that we should be kept from the tribulation. In John 17:15 He prays "I do not ask that you take them out of the world *(so no rapture)*, but that you keep them from the evil one." To be kept from the evil one is to give wisdom, insight and strength so as to recognise the temptation or deception and to be able to resist with perseverance. The word 'to be kept' in Rev. 3:10 has the same meaning, "Because you have kept my word about patient endurance, I will *keep* you from the hour of trial that is coming on the whole world, to try those who dwell on the earth." Then the Lord will powerfully stand by those who are in great distress, until He comes. So, an escape theory cannot be based on Rev. 3:10.

Especially in the darkest hour the believers will have to shine as lights on a candlestick.

ONLY ONE RETURN

We should not distinguish two phases in the return of Jesus, the first in secret, 'as a thief in the night', to take the church away, and the second with 'great power and glory' to come and be physically present to reign.

The expression 'to come as a thief' 1 Thess. 5:2, 4; 2 Pet. 3:10; Mt. 24:43; Rev. 3:3; 16:15, pertains to the unexpectedness and the suddenness of His coming. Therefore, there is a call to be watchful.

The expression 'coming with great power and glory' refers to the tremendous majesty and preponderance of Jesus over all power and authority. Both expressions refer to the same event; the one-and-only return of Jesus. He comes at the time of the breaking loose of the cosmic catastrophes to take home those who are left, together with those who have died in Christ, 1 Thess. 4:17; Mt. 24:29-31. When Jesus speaks about His coming, He uses both expressions for the same event; Mt. 24:43 and 30. So, no two phases in His return.

When Peter writes about the day of Jesus' coming, the day of the great cosmic catastrophes, then he also uses the expression 'as a thief'. That is certainly not meant as being hidden or quietly when the heavens and the earth pass away. It therefore also concerns the same coming at the end of time.

THE BRIDE

How would it be possible, as propounded by those who hold to the teaching of escape, that the raptured church is celebrating in heaven while the world is overcome by the great tribulation? Jesus wept for Jerusalem, because they did not receive Him; Lk. 19:41-44; Mt. 23:37. Would He still not be weeping because of His continual rejection and of all the suffering that would overtake them? And would the Gentile Christian community not feel the same sorrow and great anguish, Rom. 9:1-5, as long as Israel is *abandoned*, because they chose the wrong way?

Celebrating the wedding feast in heaven without Israel?

In the first place, isn't Israel destined to be the bride? Hos. 2:16, 19, 20.

Specifically, because Israel is the *unfaithful* bride, the Gentile Christian church will be used to provoke her to jealousy. To wit, the Lord will provoke them to jealousy by what He will do in and with the church, so that Israel will perceive the Bridegroom-Bride relationship between the Lord and the church and will start to long for Him. A raptured church will never be able to provoke Israel to jealousy. The Gentile Christian church together with Israel will be the bride. Together we will become one olive tree. Together we will be one flock under one Shepherd. We may not make a separation where the Lord specifically desires to make us one. He has consigned all, Israel as well as the Gentiles, to disobedience, in order that He may have mercy on all; Rom. 11:32

In the eternal kingdom the wedding feast will be celebrated in unison by the faithful ones from Jew and Gentile, after judgment has been passed on the unfaithful ones from Jew and Gentile, the 'great harlot' of Rev. 19, the followers of the beast.

So, the judgment over the great harlot cannot fall before Israel has turned to the Lord, but who yet later will once again fall away, for it is especially Israel who is depicted in Scripture as the whore; Jer. 3 and Ezek. 16.

Jesus too acknowledges Israel as the bride, although in a negative sense: "...an adulterous generation", Mt. 12:39.

We must serve in the bridal-gaining of Israel.

WHAT RESTRAINS THE LAWLESS ONE?

In escape theology the Holy Spirit is seen as the One who restrains the lawless one of 2 Thess. 2, Who first must be removed before the lawless one is revealed. The Holy Spirit Who dwells in the church, will return to heaven when the church is raptured. This interpretation is needed in order to place the rapture of the church before the great tribulation. Or to put it in other words: because of the notion that the rapture takes place before the tribulation, they come to this exegesis. Then the expectation is that when the lawless one oppresses all of humanity, a number of Jews will turn to the Lord.

How will Israel repent and turn to the Lord if the Holy Spirit along with the church has left for heaven? The Holy Spirit is the One who must convict of sin, because they have not believed in Jesus, John 16:8-10, and He is the One who leads into all truth. How will those Jews who are awaiting the Messiah be convinced that He *has already come*, and that it is the righteousness of God that He *now is with the Father*, and they no longer must expect Him physically on earth but must expect Him to dwell in their hearts?

If the salt of the earth, the church, has left, revival and conversion no longer is possible, but instead death and destruction will advance.

So, no rapture before the lawless one is revealed, nor before the conversion of Israel. The Holy Spirit never can be the one Who restrains and then is taken away, for Jesus says that the Holy Spirit will remain forever; John 14:16.

In Rev. 7:1-3 there is talk of an angel who comes from the rising of the sun, who has the seal of God. His job is to seal the servants of God on their foreheads. He *restrains* four angels, who will execute judgment affecting all of the world, or in other words, who will smite the earth with a curse.

Before the judgments really break lose and the earth is smitten with a curse, the Lord will, through an elianic action, give Israel and the nations one more chance to accept Him as Lord and King.

When the heart of present day Israel has been brought back to the hearts of the patriarchs and when the estrangement of faith that grew between modern Judaism and the faith of the ancient fathers is lifted, when Israel will realise that the heavenly Father indeed did provide on Golgotha a Lamb for sacrifice, then this ancient, chosen people will be *sealed* with the Holy Spirit.

Whoever believes in atonement through the sacrificial blood shed on Golgotha will also be sealed with the Holy Spirit; Eph. 1:13; Eph. 4:30b.

This sealing reminds us of the blood sign on the posts of the doors in Egypt. When Israel hides under the blood of the Passover Lamb, they will experience a passing over of the angel of death. Then the curse passes by for now; the angels holding back the four winds may not harm the earth as yet; there will be a delay of the judgments. Upon Israel's repentance and turning back the Kingdom of God will break through. The gospel of the Kingdom will resound throughout all the earth, among all nations; Mt. 24:14

The task of the angel ascending from the rising of the sun, Rev. 7:2, coincides with the task of the angel with a face like the sun, Rev. 10:1.

After the Millennium, at the apostasy, there will be *no more delay*, Rev. 10:6, then the four angels of the four winds will no longer be *restrained* and the last judgments will break lose, because then the lawless one will establish his dictatorship on earth.

What is it that keeps the lawless one from revealing himself today? *First* Israel must except the Lamb of God, the crucified One. *First* the Kingdom of God must break through. *First* all promises concerning Israel's restoration must be fulfilled. *First* grace must have been offered to all nations; Mt. 24:14.

Then the son of perdition will find opportunity to infiltrate the church and to set himself in the temple of God. He only can set himself in that temple when that temple from Jew and Gentile has been restored. However, at the coming of Jesus he will be defeated; 2 Thess. 2:8.

Paul knew of the turning of Israel that the Lord would bring about. He longed for this. Of course, he also did speak about this with the Thessalonians. Therefore, he could write concerning the lawless one: "And you know what is restraining him now so that he may be revealed in his time."

FULLNESS IS NOT A NUMBER

The escape and two-phase teaching is also demonstrated from Rom. 11:25, 26, where it says: "Lest you be wise in your own sight, I do not want you to be unaware of this mystery, brothers: a partial hardening has come upon Israel, until the fullness of the Gentiles has come in."

The hardening of Israel lasts until the fullness of the Gentiles has come in. *Fullness* does not mean a full or certain number that enters heaven. Romans 11 does not speak at all about heaven, nor about the rapture. Just as the word *'until'*, *'coming in'* has more to do with time. God has fixed the times and seasons in His own authority, Acts 1:6, 7, also concerning the restoration of the kingdom to Israel. Israel will be saved because the fullness of the Gentiles will break through, will come in.

A certain number of Gentile believers taken up into heaven will never provoke Israel to jealousy. A raptured church cannot contribute to Israel's salvation. A fixed number that is taken up into heaven does diminish God's love and righteousness, as if the next child of God then has some bad luck, not being able to go to heaven, because the number is filled up.

The word *fullness* in Rom. 11:25 has the same meaning as the word *fullness* in Eph. 4:10 and 13. Jesus will *bring all to fullness, will fulfil all things*. The church must come to maturity, to the fullness of Christ. Therefore, the fullness of the Gentiles holds in that the Lord will bring the church to her full destiny, to wit, that His workings in the church will become recognisable; that the church will be conformed to the image of Christ; Rom. 8:29; and will function as a people for His Name; Acts 15:14.

'And in this way', or in this manner Israel will see Jesus and will turn and be saved. Romans 11 speaks of the function of the Gentile Christian church vis-à-vis Israel. The Lord will use us to provoke Israel to jealousy, Rom. 11:11, He has shown us mercy, so that Israel now too will receive mercy, Rom. 11:31. He will bring us to fullness so that all Israel will be saved; Rom. 11:25, 26. The Lord wants to unite us in the one olive tree upon which believing Israel will be regrafted; Rom. 11:23. He will have mercy on both of us; Rom. 11:32.

HUNDRED FORTY-FOUR THOUSAND

If one wants to understand the concept of 'the fullness of the Gentiles' quantitatively, do you then also interpret the concept of the 'fullness of Israel' that way? Would that fullness then represent the one hundred forty-four thousand from the book of Revelation?

The fullness of Israel is simply Israel *coming to her destiny* through the *fulfilling action* of Jesus. Rom. 11:26 teaches us that all Israel will be saved, and not just one hundred forty-four thousand.

The book of Revelation uses so much symbolic language that we must be careful not to always take the numbers literally. The number one hundred forty-four thousand (that is twelve times twelve times one thousand, or three times four times ten times ten times ten) is full of symbolism. It means, the 'full number according to God's measure', *all* of the people, *all* God's children, the *totality* of God's elect.

By taking this number literally we very much short-change the overwhelming love, power and majesty of our Lord.

Would He only be able to convert one hundred forty-four thousand Jews? That would only be one percent of the present number of Jews.

The blood of the lambs applied to the doorposts in Egypt delivered at least six hundred thousand Israelites from the power of Pharaoh! Would the blood of Jesus only be able to save but a quarter of that number from Satan's power? Is the blood of Jesus of less value than the lambs' blood in Egypt? Or has God's power become diminished? Is Jesus smaller than Satan?

In the Second World War Satan was able to destroy six million Jews, one-third of the total Jewish population of that time. That is ten times as many as the number delivered from Egypt. Is Jesus then no match for Satan that He is not even able to save 2.5 percent (144,000) of the six million victims of the Holocaust from the remaining two-third of the leftover Jews?

That is pretty narrow-minded! Indeed, a very insulting teaching! Jesus purchases with His precious, holy and divine blood all Israel; more, much more than what Satan has destroyed! And certainly much more than one hundred forty-four thousand!

The one hundred forty-four thousand of Rev. 7 do not only concern the people of Israel. That the tribes are mentioned in a mixed order, that some tribes are not mentioned, and others are mentioned twice, does mean that it is not only about Israel, but that it concerns the whole community of Jew and Gentile together. All those who have been grafted into Israel are included into this; Ps. 87:6. It concerns the church that hides under the blood of the Passover Lamb. They are sealed with His blood and with His Holy Spirit. Whoever is sealed, is certainly saved! It concerns here the church before the millennial kingdom of peace.

By naming the tribes of Israel, God respects Israel's high position, Israel's election. Israel is and remains representative. The one hundred forty-four thousand in Rev. 14 again deal with the whole community of Jew and Gentile, but here it is before the breakthrough of the eternal kingdom, so, after the millennial kingdom of peace. They are described as virginal. This in contrast to the apostate Christianity of those days, who will be unfaithful to the Lord, who will fornicate and are described as the great harlot. The faithful church is virginal, the bride of the Lamb, Rev. 19:7. They have the Name of the Father and of the Son on their foreheads, Rev. 14:1. This in contrast to the apostates, who carry the mark and the name of the beast. These one hundred forty-four thousand of the end times of Rev. 14 are the same group as those depicted as the 'great multitude' in Rev. 7, who have come out of the great tribulation. Therefore, John first sees in Rev. 7 the true church of before the millennium and then the true church of just before the coming of the eternal kingdom, after the millennial kingdom of peace.

COMING WITH THE SAINTS

The doctrine of escape teaches us that Jesus physically comes to earth to reign. He will come with great power and glory. And He will come with all the saints. Those saints are equated with the raptured church returning to earth to reign with Christ.

Paul writes in 1 Thess. 3:13 that our Lord Jesus will come with all His saints. If we read the end of chapter 3 in connection with what he writes concerning the coming of the Lord in chapter 4, then we have to conclude that Jesus will bring with Him all those who have fallen asleep, 1 Thess. 4:14 "For since we believe that Jesus died and rose again, even so, through Jesus, God will bring with him those who have fallen asleep."

So, 'all His saints' in 1 Thess. 3:13 must therefore be the saints who have passed away and are 'at home with the Lord', and now will return for the resurrection, in order to arise with a glorified body together with those who are alive and left and be caught up together in the clouds, so to be always with the Lord. The resurrection precedes the rapture. Therefore, the saints from 1 Thess. 3:13 cannot have been caught up or raptured prior to this.

According to 1 Thess. 4:14-16 those saints or holy ones from 1 Thess. 3:13 could be those who have died in Christ, but if we compare this with 2 Thess. 1:7, then Paul also could be alluding to the angels, who will accompany Jesus at His coming. "…when the Lord Jesus is revealed from heaven with his mighty angels."

Jesus too tells us that He will come with His angels, whom He will send out to separate the evil from the righteous; Mt. 13:41, 49.

Therefore, at Jesus' coming we may expect with Him those who have fallen asleep as well as the angels. But not believers who would have already been raptured.

MARTYRS AS KINGS

In the millennial kingdom of peace Jesus reigns through His Spirit. But in Rev. 20 supposedly the proposition is made that the martyrs, "the souls of those who had been beheaded for the testimony of Jesus and for the word of God, and those who had not worshiped the beast or its image and had not received its mark on their foreheads or their hands" will reign with Christ for a thousand years.

In the first place this text, Rev. 20:4, contradicts the teaching of escape. These 'souls' have not been spared tribulation.

But they are the martyrs from the period after the millennium. They are the blood-witnesses of the last years before the end of our transitory dispensation. They are the oppressed saints of the true church during the time of Satan's release.

How then could they reign for a thousand years?

The Lord uses here a metaphor that He has used before. To wit, He sees people whom He regards highly as representative and attributes something to them what they have not done, or from a time in which they definitely did not live.

For example, Jesus ascribes the guilt of the shed blood of Abel to the Jewish people, while in Abel's time there were no Jews at all; Mt. 23:35. This He does because He acknowledges Israel in her high calling and election, and therefore He holds her accountable.

Another example is found in Rev. 13:8 [NKJV]. There John writes concerning the "Lamb slain from the foundation of the world." How is that possible? Wasn't Jesus crucified forty centuries after Adam! Yes. And yet…. The Father esteems His Son so highly and representative for all of mankind that He already applies Jesus' atoning suffering and death to before the foundation of the world. As if the sacrifice on Golgotha then already had occurred. Although Jesus had not yet brought this offer, His death on the cross already had effect from the time of Adam and Eve, the dawning of mankind.

Rev. 20:4 must be read in the same manner. To the martyr church of the last days symbolically is given the right, peace and blessings of the millennial kingdom of peace, as if they did control that time, did reign then, while they did not live at that time at all. But with this the Lord acknowledges them as firstfruits, Rev. 14:4, as representatives.

When Jesus stands before Caiaphas, He says: "But from now on the Son of Man shall be seated at the right hand of the power of God." Jesus, although at that time He was the accused, the one who would be judged, sees Himself as the Judge seated at the right hand of God.

In a similar way He shows to John that they "who follow the Lamb wherever he goes", Rev. 14:4, those who are truly one with Christ, also in His suffering, are judged, beheaded, but as He Himself they are judges and do reign. "Authority to judge was committed to them", Rev. 20:4. They are the judges while they were being judged.

The martyrs have not loved their lives unto death, and therefore they receive from God this acknowledgment.

This re-evaluation must encourage and comfort them when they suffer in the great tribulation. They are martyrs, but the Lord calls them kings. This depiction of things, this symbolism, shows *how* God evaluates them. It looks like they are the losers, but the Lord declares them victorious.

It is as if the Lord says to them: 'Your suffering is so valuable to Me, that I see you as kings and judges, although you feel you are the martyrs. All of the millennial kingdom of peace I see as a retroactive result of your suffering.'

The Lord gives this comforting vision before telling of Satan's final action in Rev. 20:8, the action of the beastlike figures, to whom these faithful Christians will not bow.

REVERSAL

Martyrs are seen by the Lord as kings, whereas the political and religious leaders of that time are disdainfully labelled as beasts. But this reversed qualification should not surprise us, for we do meet this more than once in the Bible. "Whoever would be great among you must be your servant, and whoever would be first among you must be your slave." Mt. 20:26, 27;

23:11. "Whoever humbles himself like this child is the greatest in the kingdom of heaven." Mt. 23:12

God called Israel, this nation of slaves, His "hosts" or His "armies"! [NKJV] Ex. 7:4. Gideon thought of himself as being a weakling, but the Angel of the Lord called him a mighty man of valour; Judges 6:12.

"But many who are first will be last, and the last first." Mt. 19:30. Therefore the last saints of the end time are called by Jesus the firstfruits. Rev. 14:4.

RESURRECTION, BUT NOT IN STAGES

So also this reversal: "Whoever finds his life will lose it, and whoever loses his life for my sake will find it." Mt. 10:39. The martyrs of Rev. 20 in principal already share in the resurrection. "Do not be surprised, brothers, that the world hates you. We know that we have passed out of death into life…" 1 John 3:13, 14.

"Truly, truly, I say to you, whoever hears my word and believes him who sent me has eternal life. He does not come into judgment, but has passed from death to life." John 5:24.

In this spiritual sense John writes in his gospel, John 5:24, as well as in his first letter, 1 John 3:14, and in the book of Revelation, Rev. 20:4-6.

Paul too writes that we were dead, but now do live; Rom. 6:13. This is valid for *every* believer. However, the Lord underlines this especially for these last persecuted believers. They are especially reminded that all those who have died with Christ, who have been crucified with Him, do also partake in His resurrection and life; Rom. 6:4, 6, 13 2 Tim. 2:11, 12. John writes: "This is the first resurrection", so to accentuate in the first place that especially they have risen and live. This does not exclude that this life is also for all other believers.

Consider that nowhere in the Bible mention is made of a second resurrection. When symbolically mention is made of the first resurrection, then this points to the fact that the martyrs of the short, halfway interrupted time are valued and acknowledged as firstfruits to God.

Those who have partaken of this first resurrection or who have been born again, will not come into judgment, John 5:24, or said differently: the second death has no power over them, Rev. 20:6. These texts can be laid next to each other. They concern the same thing.

That the judgment of the lake of fire, Rev. 20:14, is called the second death, should teach us that this is not speaking of a biological death and likewise that the first resurrection is not a biological rising either.

Together all will arise from a biological death 'on the last day', as Jesus calls it. Therefore, we should not think of the resurrection in stages.

STARTING POINT

When Rev. 20:4 is taken literally and from that text confirmation is sought elsewhere in the Bible, then certainly things will go awry and Scriptures will be taken out of context. We already have given some examples of this. Rom. 11:25, 26, nor Rev. 3:10, Zech. 13:6 and 2 Thess. 2:6-8 do support different stages in the return of Christ and the rapture, if they are not taken out of context.

The many symbols of the book of Revelation should not be just taken literally, when the Bible does not give any further clues for such a literal approach.

It would be better to take the clear portions of Scripture as a starting point and from there interpret the more difficult portions about the same subject. And yes, the Holy Spirit will convincingly answer our prayers for clarity.

PRIESTLY SERVICE

The 'escape doctrine' is very attractive and gratifies the flesh. How great not to have to suffer persecution! And then later to reign with Christ!

From Old Testament prophecies the Jewish people drew the conclusion that they would reign with the Messiah at the head of all nations.

But Jesus is not such a King. His kingdom is not of this world; John 18:36. Neither will Israel have a dominating role, but contrariwise Israel must have a serving function. Israel must be a nation of priests among the other nations; Ex. 19:6; Isa. 61:6.

When the disciples, coming from this carnal Jewish viewpoint, hope for a nice government job, and missus Zebedee asks Jesus for a position for both her boys at the side of Jesus, then Jesus totally corrects her. It is not about reigning or exercising power, but about serving; Mt. 20:25-28. Specifically, in serving the greatest influence is exercised.

Neither should we entertain such carnal expectations as to once reign as kings. We must be willing to serve. We should long to be one with Christ, even if that means to suffer with Him. In this way we too may serve as priests.

The firstfruits are great to God because of their total surrender to Him. The martyrs — the doormats, the slaves, the vilified and abused, rejected, humiliated and killed — they are the ones who are promoted by the Lord! Their serving is what influences the world. They are the priests before God; Rev. 20:6.

Whoever thinks that the Jews will be the valets — as is alleged by a variant of the two-way doctrine — of those kings who will reign in the millennial kingdom of peace, should read Isa. 61:5, 6, where it is stated:

"Strangers shall stand and tend your *(i.e. Israel's)* flocks; foreigners shall be your plowmen and vinedressers; but you shall be called the priests of the Lord; they shall speak of you as the ministers of our God." So, Israel will not become the valet. On the contrary, Israel will be clothed with a very exalted calling, the calling of being priests, as was already determined at the making of the covenant in Ex. 19:6. We Christians do have the same intercessory function as far as we are grafted into Israel. This function means: proclaiming and making peace, teaching and reconciling, bringing salvation and speaking rightly, bringing advise on behalf of the Lord through the Holy Spirit. Even if that would result into suffering. For we must be of the same mind as Christ, Who freely emptied Himself of His glory and died as a slave for us; Phil. 2:5-8.

And just because of His death as the sacrificial lamb Jesus may implement God's plan of government; Rev. 5:6-14. Jesus went into His glory at the Ascension. Now He reigns with the Father on the throne. To the church of the end times it is true in the first place that those who conquer "I will grant him to sit with me on my throne", Rev. 3:21. That is not in an earthly manner, but in the heavenly Kingdom, where Jesus is seated in the throne of the Father. Let us think more of serving than of possibly reigning at some time. With this we may show to be followers of Jesus in His mindset.

EPILOGUE

One day the Lord will come! We must keep on expecting Him. In the first place in our own lives.

But let us not just be interested in those last days and forget what still necessarily must happen before Jesus comes.

We expect the breakthrough of the Kingdom of God as soon as Israel acknowledges Jesus as Saviour. However, Israel will not perceive that Jesus is her Messiah as long as the Gentile Christian church remains divided and keeps on devouring each other, and so Israel will not get a true picture of Jesus.

It is to us to humble ourselves, to confess our guilt concerning our divisions and arrogance to Israel and each other. It is to us to become one with God the Father and God the Son, so that we will acknowledge each other as Christians, regardless of our labels. We must be willing to remember together the death of our Lord, without first asking: are you a member of my church? The Spirit will make us willing to do this in a time of great distress.

And so, on that united proclamation, the Spirit will intervene in such a manner that Jesus will be glorified and will be recognised and acknowledged by Israel! That truly is the sanctification of His Name! Then God's Kingdom will break through in fullness here on earth.

May the Lord give an opening and understanding for this expectation.

To Him be the glory and the honour and the power forever and ever. Amen.